You're Invited to a Country Wedding!

A stunning bride in a white dress and boots...dashing cowboys in blue jeans and black hats...an outdoor aisle lined with brilliant garden flowers...the creak of wagon wheels...the clip-clop of horses' hooves.

Those sights and sounds of a country-style wedding, plus many more, come to vivid life in the pages of this one-of-a-kind volume. If you, too, want a friendly, less formal "hitchin' " that reflects rural values and a hardworking, fun-loving lifestyle, this is the book for you!

We've lassoed a unique collection of ideas from the readers of *Country Woman* magazine to help you (or someone you love) plan a delightfully memorable day.

Photo Opportunity

As you turn the pages of this uniquely *country* brides' book, you'll feel as if you're peeking inside hundreds of wedding albums and chatting with the brides and grooms to find out how they made their big day practical yet special, casual yet lovely.

Scores of colorful photos detail what the happy couples and their attendants wore...the settings and decorations for their ceremonies and receptions...and more.

Bridal Buffet

Right at your fingertips, too, are more than 50 delicious down-home recipes for a country bridal buffet—from appealing appetizers and beverages to main dishes, breads, salads, hot sides and homemade desserts. It's a banquet sure to satisfy your guests' heartiest appetites.

Also on the menu is a showstopping wedding cake with horsehoe layers that's sure to be the center of attention—and you won't have to hire a caterer to make it!

Handmade Heirlooms

If you're hoping to add handmade accents or heirlooms to your big day, you'll find all kinds of creative ideas here. Included are instructions for over 35 crafts—from bridal bouquets, ring pillows and cake toppers to table decor, fast favors and more.

We've even come up with our own gorgeous simple-to-sew wedding gown—you can make it for *under $100!* You won't find the pattern anywhere but here.

So why not "sit a spell" and page through this idea-packed guidebook for country brides? You're sure to find a wagon-load of ideas to put to use when you (or some folks close to you) tie the knot!

Down the Aisle Country-Style

Executive Editor: Kathy Pohl
Managing Editor: Faithann Stoner
Food Editor: Janaan Cunningham
Associate Food Editor: Coleen Martin
Senior Recipe Editor: Sue A. Jurack
Recipe Editor: Janet Briggs
Test Kitchen Home Economist: Mary Beth Jung
Craft Editors: Jane Craig, Tricia Coogan
Associate Editors: Sharon Selz, Kathleen Anderson,
Julie Kastello, Ann Kaiser, Jean Steiner
Editorial Assistants: Joanne Wied, Sarah Grimm
Art Director & Illustrator: Vicky Marie Moseley
Assistant Art Director: Tom Hunt
Photographers: Scott Anderson, Dan Roberts,
Glenn Thiesenhusen
Food Photography Artist: Stephanie Marchese
Photo Studio Manager: Anne Schimmel
Production Assistants: Claudia Wardius, Ellen Lloyd

© 2000 Reiman Publications, LLC
5400 S. 60th Street, Greendale WI 53129

International Standard Book Number: 0-89821-283-9
Library of Congress Catalog Card Number: 99-76346

Cowboy Weds Cinderella

THE smiling newlyweds on our cover are Keith and Brook Hickle of Enumclaw, Washington.

"After a year-long courtship, Keith got down on one knee and proposed to me during a romantic horseback ride," Brook details. "Of course, I said yes!

"Ever since I was little, I knew that I wanted a wedding at home—and my folks were happy to oblige. Our Western-themed ceremony was held on their front lawn in front of a flower-filled buckboard."

While her cowboy sported casual attire, Brook walked down a country aisle wearing the dress of her dreams, created by a talented aunt.

"She was my fairy godmother! Making that dress was a year-long labor of love. When I wore it on my wedding day, I felt just like Cinderella," Brook recalls with a radiant smile.

"Our pictures were taken by a high school teacher of mine—Peter La Pointe—who has his own studio called Focal Point Photography. We were so pleased with how they turned out. Every time we look at them, it's like reliving that beautiful day all over again."

Step Inside...

Beautiful Brides & Gallant Grooms

Combining their love for each other and the great outdoors, these newlyweds pledged their "I do's" in true country-style— under blue skies...or with other rural ties.

GETTING IN THE SWING of marriage was easy for Darren and Theresa Hinen. Reveals his mom, Jeri, of Soap Lake, Washington, "They're truly country. They exchanged vows in our farmyard and had a reception in the new log barn. An antique wagon held gifts."

A PEAK EXPERIENCE for her daughter Kari Lynn and Terry Byvank was tying the knot on a mountaintop, says Laurine Marquette of Westlock, Alberta. The bride's muff kept the chills away.

SIMPLY HAPPY are longtime friends Pam and Gordon Taylor of Fort Wayne, Indiana. They wore their favorite overalls to get hitched on her parents' farm October 12, their mutual birthday.

MILES OF SMILES turned up when Tammy and Steve Didier held a festive Western wedding on his family's ranch. "We didn't want a stuffy gathering," tells Tammy of Elk City, Idaho. "We designed our own country-style invitations and cake topper and asked guests to dress casually. My mom and his dad stood up with us."

LAWFULLY JOINED. Cheryl and Ron Schaefer of Bull Valley, Illinois love ranching, so Ron and their "posse" of attendants wore sheriff's badges instead of flowers.

BUILT ON LOVE. Lorra Rhyner and Mark Sleger were married under a hickory tree in their Poynette, Wisconsin field near the log home they built. Their picnic reception included a hog roast.

A HISTORY TOGETHER. Their passion for the past led Carla and Reyes Rich of Moss, Tennessee to marry in a century-old church amid the mountains. "As we drove around the scenic valley afterward, a bear joined our wedding party," the bride remembers.

SOMETHING OLD, SOMETHING NEW. Antiques surrounded Cheyenne and Paul Winkler when they were wed in a Western museum in Spearfish, South Dakota. The bride's deerskin dress was designed by her aunt. A cowboy poet wrote a special tribute.

SPLASHY EVENT. Ed Shramek of Powell, Wyoming walks on water in his new wife Jill's eyes! Their outdoor ceremony was held at a gorgeous resort near a river.

More Brides and Grooms...

RURAL ROMANCE reigned at the ranch wedding of Krista and Tony Reed. "My mom and sisters designed colorful flower boxes to trim the wedding deck and hanging baskets for the reception in a machine shop," Krista, from Ellensburg, Washington, offers.

WOODED BLISS. Her groom picked a sylvan site on his family's farm years before they met, says bride KC Bobolz of Oak Creek, Wisconsin. "The guests were driven to our 'chapel in the woods' by carriage along a scenic trail marked with ribboned trees."

LOVE AND MARRIAGE coupled with a horse-drawn carriage assured Allison and Wayne McKinnon of getting carried away with a wedding on a working guest ranch. "The altar featured bales topped with antiques," she pens from Carseland, Alberta.

COMPATIBLE OVERALL. Cute twosome Lee and Robert Balcom from Benton City, Washington dressed the part for their farm-focused wedding. Accenting matching bibs, shirts and straw hats were a sunflower bouquet plus a new pitchfork.

GOING WITH THEIR GRAIN is a favorite wedding photograph of David and Linda Code from rural Carbon, Alberta. Taken in a neighbor's field, it shows the newlywed farm partners knee-deep in barley…and love.

HOMESPUN NUPTIALS were a labor of love for Amy and Michael Kennedy and families. The bride's mother made the dresses while the groom's sister created invitations and a beeswax unity candle. "Michael and I built a latticed arch and wooden lanterns for our setting," adds Amy of Elmwood, Nebraska.

CUPID'S LASSO led ranchers Naomi and Philip Schellenberg of Cochrane, Alberta to tie the knot country-style. "I do's" were followed by a reception in a mountaintop ski chalet decked with saddles, hay bales, boots and bridles. A well-versed MC recited cowboy poetry to strains of Western music.

WESTERN UNION of her daughter Becky and Mike Bell was a truly historic occasion, shares Cheryl Klotz of Bonney Lake, Washington. "The ceremony was set in a historical village straight out of pioneer days."

Flowers & Frills

*Carrying homegrown bouquets and donning everything
from lovely lace to down-home denim dresses,
these wedding parties looked as pretty as their country settings!*

"PLAIN" PERFECT. "Amanda Irvine graced the windswept plains of Wyoming to marry our son Neal," notes Nancy Sorenson of Arvada. "She wore an eggplant-colored velvet gown trimmed with silver studs and buttons and carried lilies."

"TWO" CUTE. "Our son, Darcy, wed Pamela Westerlund on the open range, so naturally her flower girl cousins dressed in prairie-style skirts," smiles Lorna Gorgichuk of Willingdon, Alberta. Western vests topped their homemade outfits.

Images by Allison

HIGH-STEPPING. Country line dancing brought Chris and Sue Armstrong of Auburndale, Florida together. Says Chris, "Sue's dress included fabric from a favorite lace tablecloth. I added the band and veil to her hat. Sue's daughters stood up in dresses with white fringe, hats and boots. My Western tux and her boots came just in time for our vows at a historic fort. Fresh flowers were a lovely touch."

SOMETHING OLD, SOMETHING NEW. Tara McLain of Bluejacket, Oklahoma told Keith "I do" in an antique ivory lace gown with satin underlay, crocheted lace, a beaded bodice and satin rosettes on the sleeves. Her silk rose bouquet included four handkerchiefs, one from each of her great-grandmothers. The bridesmaids had burgundy skirts and floral-print vests, and the flower girl wore a matching pinafore.

PRETTY IN PINK (AND BLUE). "Alisa and Eric Boatwright's attendants made their coordinating dresses with denim tops and mauve cotton and lace skirts," reports cousin Joy Dennis from Venice, Utah. "They carried silk flowers in the same colors. Alisa bought her Western dress, then added a lacy train. Her hat trailed a veil in back."

COUNTRY ELEGANCE. "For Angela and Lonnie Robertson's nuptials, the bridesmaids wore simple country-style floral-print dresses and straw hats with matching bands," report Angela's parents, Blaz and Gertrude Gojmerac of Souris, Prince Edward Island. "A neighbor stitched Angela's lace and satin gown, and they carried fresh bouquets."

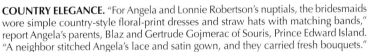

LOVE "REINS". Mindy Owens rode into the arena on horseback in a satin gown with beaded shawl and fringe to marry Chad Holmes in Loranger, Louisiana. Her cowboy hat had pearls and a veil. He wore a turquoise shirt with Southwestern border, black jeans and a hat. Her silk bouquet captured the wedding colors.

A BIG BOUQUET of just-picked wildflowers was carried by Vicki French of Edgewood, New Mexico. She chose the site of an old Spanish ruins for her marriage to Ryan…and wore her mom's 30-year-old wedding dress, white boots and a banded white hat.

OH SOW ROMANTIC were the nostalgic sweet peas Kristina Schweitzer's mother seeded for her and her husband Troy's wedding. "We used them for bridal flowers, as accents for the cake and in cowboy boot vases on the tables," the bride writes from Dawson Creek, British Columbia. "My brocade gown was just as old-fashioned, with the same Venice lace that trimmed my bridesmaids' denim dresses. The guys wore black Wranglers and vests."

PRETTY POSE shows the elegant side of country bride Jennie Braley and her attending sisters, Jessica (far left) and Jamie. "Jennie's horse hardly recognized her in her flouncy layers of satin and lace," grins Jennie's mother, Ruth Tidwell of Veyo, Utah. "Her groom Pat's aunt arranged the bouquets and bark baskets."

HARVEST HUES colored Debbie and Bruce Palmer's "I do's". "Wildflowers tucked into bandannas tied in with the bridesmaids' broomstick skirts and denim shirts," says Debbie from Alice, North Dakota. "I chose a fringed Western dress...and a leafy head wreath instead of a traditional bouquet to leave my hands free for riding my horse."

FRESH AS THE DAISIES picked for her bright-eyed bouquets are Brandy Gibbs and her bevy of bridesmaids. "The daisy print in the girls' skirts was set off by red vests," elaborates the bride from Eureka, Nevada, where she and Matt live.

SWEET 'N' SIMPLE farm wedding struck the fancy of Teresa Stauffer and her groom, Nelson, of Lambertville, New Jersey. Her beaded tea-length dress and attendant Andrea Hoke's gingham are as timeless as their silk flower bouquets.

ROUNDING UP ROSES in lassos gave a Western twist to the wedding of LaVon and Ron Stoppleworth from Gwinner, North Dakota. "Ron's mom made the fringed satin gowns for my daughter and her niece," writes the proud mother-of-the-bride, Sharon Shockley.

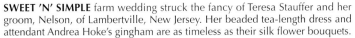

CUPID CRAFTED the attraction between her and groom Dennis, but Yvette Sparks of Orange, Texas did the rest. "I designed my bustled dress, the gals' frilly patchwork skirts and their heart-shaped baskets."

A FRINGE BENEFIT for Ruth Wilson was designing her gown. She "laced up" a tan denim skirt and a blue silk bodice. Blooms graced the arch where she joined hearts with Ward in Graham, Washington.

Scenic Settings

These happy couples celebrated their wedding day in a country way—in picturesque places with special rustic touches that made for one-of-a-kind ceremonies!

Rachael Jenkins

RUSTIC AND ROMANTIC. The rural Kokomo, Indiana home of Becky Oyler was the site of son Scott and Amanda's wedding. With corn fields as a backdrop, they exchanged vows in front of a frame made from barn siding. Fence rails and wagon wheels added to the ambiance.

SHADY GLADE. For her ceremony, daughter Angie and Mike Conrad chose a secluded spot on a high school campus, tells Lorrie Stoltzfus of Lancaster, Pennsylvania. Straw bales, shepherd's crooks with bows and hanging plants lined the aisle.

Rick Titus

Grove Studio

"SHORE-LY" HAPPY are Linda and Creighton Cox of Embarrass, Minnesota. They said their vows at a lovely lake in June beneath an iron gazebo that the groom made.

CIRCLE OF LOVE. With a view of rolling hills and forest, Kevin and KC Bobolz, Oak Creek, Wisconsin, tied the knot on his family's farm. The groom picked wild grapevines to form a giant wreath with a rustic cross inside. Hay bales and pretty potted plants served as the altar. Guests sat on planks laid across hay bales.

BRIGHT IDEA. Candelabras decked with flowers, the groom's hat and a lariat flanked the church altar when her daughter Janelle wed Reggie Randau, says Eileen Blom of Oskaloosa, Iowa. Afterwards, the bride presented her groom with his hat to wear down the aisle.

SIMPLE YET SPECIAL. Pines, antique farm implements and mums decorated the site of the farmyard wedding of her daughter Stacy and Clint Spells, shares Melissa Barkhimer from Camden, Arkansas. Flaming torches lined the aisle. The couple wore coordinating outfits.

"FALL" IN LOVE. The November nuptials of her daughter Shevon and Michael Zellers on the groom's father's land was accented with autumn hues, notes Linda McCale of Belton, Missouri. The pair wed under an arch twined with silk flowers.

BARNYARD BLISS. "Our daughter Gina and Erik Bjorvik wed in a farm-turned-park," pens Sharon Hoblit of Bend, Oregon. "Cream cans accented the tulle-wrapped archway."

ENCHANTING SPAN in a park served as the aisle at Kristi and Troy Martin's nuptials. "It was decked with cowboy hats trimmed with paper twist bows and rosebuds," the bride's mom, Barbara Reynolds of Brandon, Florida, reports. "Their entry song was *Love Can Build a Bridge.*"

ALTARED PLAN. Rain didn't dampen Tracey and Louis Levreault's wish to wed in the family farmyard. Instead, the Baldur, Manitoba twosome became one in front of a rural mural in the reception hall—complete with straw.

A HOMEMADE STAGE was set for a Western-style wedding when Cindy and Kent Vance joined hands on the groom's family homestead. "Our altar was a saddle and pair of milk can flower holders," the bride notes from Gill, Colorado. "Dark green hay bales were reserved for relatives, lighter bales seated friends." The table accents and wedding attire were all Cindy's handiwork.

CUPID'S CORRAL. For rodeo-loving duo Chenine and Trace Humphrey, a backyard hitching post in Aldergrove, British Columbia was an ideal spot to tie the knot. The wooden arch was brightened by sunflowers and cattails.

A CHARMING ARBOR decorated with grapevines and flowers was made by the groom's father and formed the altar at Tim and Tina Thomann's wedding. "It was transported to the ceremony site—a beautiful hillside where the couple hopes to build their future home," writes the groom's great-aunt, Shirley King from Lone Tree, Iowa.

BLUE RIBBON VENUE. The Carroll County 4-H Fair was grounds for matrimony between Laura and David Zepp of Westminster, Maryland. "Since we met there, we figured it would be nice to have our wedding in the show ring," Laura shares.

A RINGSIDE SEAT for Tami and Brad Bova's union was a rodeo arena. The family sat on bales and guests filled the grandstand, jots the bride's mom, Sandra Yost from Highlands Ranch, Colorado. The couple rode in on horseback.

AN EGGS-CELLENT SETTING fit the fun farm wedding that Pat Coffee of Kingston, Washington hatched with her husband, Cliff Durant. Their guests flocked to a chicken house festooned with flowers. The bride arrived riding in true country-style—in a front-end loader!

Rides for Brides

*Fueled by imagination and powered by love, these couples put
a unique country spin on transportation to and from the ceremony
as they took their first steps toward happily ever after.*

HAPPY TRAILS were part of the program as Leanne and Billy Waters' "bridle" party piled into a shiny new horse trailer to cruise from the candlelight ceremony to the reception hall decorated with autumn accents, writes the bride's mom, Sharon Lugdon from Costigan, Maine.

A CHARMING COMBINATION of work and romance took center stage when farmer Hubertus von Westerholt wed Juliane Srbu. A park bench on his combine was the love seat for this Palmerston, Ontario pair en route to the reception.

GRAIN TRUCK GETAWAY for Linda and Daryl Siders was a heartwarming surprise from the groom's sweet corn pickers. The sunny celebration for 180 at his Fairhaven Farm in Xenia, Ohio also featured a duet sung by the bridal couple, a hog roast in a pole barn and line dancing in a converted tool shed.

CARRIED AWAY in an old-fashioned horse-drawn carriage were Karen and Pete Holmes of Chillicothe, Ohio. "The best man and maid of honor joined us on our first journey as husband and wife," recalls Karen. "The romantic ride from our small country church ceremony to the rustic reception in an apple orchard on my folks' dairy farm was magical."

FULL STEAM AHEAD! Shelly Sahm and Greg Herbert began their life together on a hay wagon pulled by her 1915 Case steam tractor to the reception in Clay, New York.

EQUINE ESCORTS took the bride and bridesmaids in grand style to the lakeside ceremony where Mikal and David Spooner were wed on her family's North Carolina farm. "We carried our flowers on horsefly whisks wrapped in gold," says the Carthage, New York bride.

SPREADING JOY as they rode through the streets of Albert Lea, Minnesota were newlyweds Brent and Lori Krueger. The wedding party filled the John Deere manure spreader. "It was an unusual trip no one will forget," says Lori.

DREAM COME TRUE for Jamie Gurney of Odessa, Missouri was a ride to church in a white carriage. "I cried when my folks unveiled the surprise," she says. "I'd dreamt of this trip since I was little. It was a perfect way to start the special day I married David."

FOR BUTTER, FOR WORSE read the sign on the hay wagon that was transporting the bridal party of John and Janelle Greene from Springboro, Pennsylvania. Their clever "limooo" took second prize as a float in a local parade that same day!

Exceptional Receptions

*After the "I do's" are all said and done, the wedding day fun begins!
The rustic receptions of these newlyweds included tasteful table toppers,
down-home decor, crafty handmade creations and more.*

TYING THE KNOTS. Red, white and blue were the hues Kimberly and Darren Cunningham chose for their nuptials. Snappy bandannas wrapped up their color scheme around the head table in a church hall in Haslett, Michigan. Patriotic tones accented the bouquets, too. The cake was decorated with red and blue flowers, and red and blue hurricane lanterns lit up guest tables. A pack of coyotes that the groom's mother, Alana, cut out with a scroll saw sported colorful kerchiefs.

THE CANNY ACCENTS at Dianne and Paul Handsaker's celebration were antique milk cans from the bride's grandfather's dairy. "We decked them with sunflowers, tiny mums, daisies and raffia," she pens from Lena, Illinois.

IVY-TWINED pillars prettied up Barb and Karl Marksman's Appleton, Wisconsin rural gathering. Terra cotta pots abloom with colorful wildflowers topped the dining tables. Tulle-wrapped mints "sprouted" from petite pots.

BARN FULL OF CHARM had Nyla Newton and Dad dancing for joy at her and husband Paul's wedding. "After painting the walls, we draped white tulle and mini lights around the wagon wheel chandelier and barn poles," Nyla glows from Alexandria, Virginia. "Citronella candles on windowsills discouraged mosquitoes."

ROMANCE BALLOONED at Vinson and Dawn Robinson's heart-of-barn wedding party—complete with hay bales and an inflatable arch, remarks the groom's mom, Janet, from French Creek, West Virginia. "We set a farm scene with antique lanterns, iron wheels and barrels. Great-Grandfather's hog trough was filled with impatiens."

A PRIME IDEA for quenching thirst was the motorized pump that kept the punch flowing at the fairgrounds potluck put on for Carol and Brad Byron from Island City, Oregon. She jots, "Denim place mats and bandanna napkins helped set our casual decor."

WELL-WISHERS enjoyed pitching into the wishing well card holder that bride Becky Wright's husband, Gary, her dad and father-in-law crafted. Its country theme was accented with small cowboy hats and horseshoes, she writes from Independence, Missouri.

ALL CHECKED OUT was the community center where Mary Jo and Doug Bures held their reception in Odell, Nebraska. "Tablecloths, rope runners, wagon wheels and barn boards gave a rural feeling," she notes. School and barn birdhouses (Mary Jo's a teacher, Doug's a farmer) perched atop the tables were made by family.

A GIFT HORSE isn't looked at too closely, but a present-packed water trough's another matter! Married in a horse stable, Wendy and Dale Mote could hardly rein in their happiness, observes Sherry Roy, mother-of-the-bride from Faubush, Kentucky.

LOFTY AFFAIR had a casual air when Kris and Jim Oliva married on the bride's family homestead, where revelry rang from the rafters of the reception barn in Juneau, Wisconsin! "Twinkling lights reflected the couple's happy glow," Kris' mom, Judy, recalls. Walls were adorned with horse collars, scythes and old tractor seats. Heart-shaped rope chains on dining tables and grapevine wreaths tied in a country flavor.

LOVING STITCHES went into the Double Wedding Ring quilt Betty Ann Wolery from Joplin, Montana fashioned for her daughter Jane and groom Darren Beadle's head table. Lilacs, lanterns and candles cast a romantic light.

THE OUTLOOK'S ROSY for Cassie and Chad Portier as good times roll in Raceland, Louisiana. Floral swags and latticework gave a lacy look and garden-fresh flavor to the barn fete, beams the bride's mom, Debbie Chiasson.

APPLE-Y EVER AFTER. Falling in love with a harvest motif, Katherine Beth and Patrick Althouse picked an "appeeling" theme for their wedding. Candles in hollowed-out apples bobbed in buckets amid Indian corn; colorful autumn leaves blazed on guest tables. The bride picked Fayette County, Ohio fairgrounds for her reception, Mom Barbara Towler says.

A MERRY MARRIAGE. With the wedding date set close to Christmas, Stephanie and Robert Merritt of Bedford, Pennsylvania chose a country Yule theme. Evergreen boughs and clever cowboy cutouts decked the tables.

22

FARMING'S IN THE CARDS for Carolyn and Paul Turba of Elkhart Lake, Wisconsin. The card box her dairyman husband built will be a toy for their children, she pens.

A TASTE OF TEXAS was dished up on the buffet table in honor of Ricki and Butch McMillan of Anton. Friend Lisa Rogers reports, "Bluebonnets sprouted from a cowboy boot, and the slow cooker was pocketed in blue jeans. Boot-handled knives spurred Texas-size smiles."

A ROMANTIC CANOPY assured that Allison and Mark Mains had a wedding day made in the shade. "Allison, who's a florist, created a budding wonderland," says the groom's mom, Sarah Jo, from New Egypt, New Jersey. Her pretty topiaries graced the lace-covered tables.

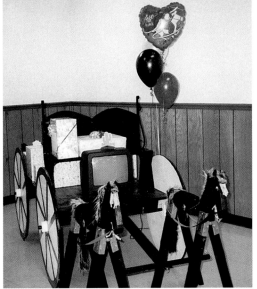

PULLING TOGETHER a gift wagon with a Western accent took teamwork on the part of Shonda and James Musselwhite of Thurmont, Maryland. The buckboard held a TV showing a video of the newlyweds from childhood.

LOADS OF LUCK was wished to Steve and Tammy Didier from Elk City, Idaho, along with a wagonful of wedding-day surprises. "My father-in-law's horse-drawn wagon looked festive with fresh paint and bright balloons," the bride explains how the past became part of their presents.

HATS OFF to Ron and Cheryl Schaefer, who put their heads together on homespun nuptials. "A friend made the papier-mache cowboy hat—complete with a card slot in the crown," Cheryl, from Bull Valley, Illinois, jots. "We built a cedar corral/hitching post where we exchanged vows."

23

Country Bridal Buffet...

APPEALING APPETIZERS AND BEST BEVERAGES!
Clockwise from top left: Lime Sherbet Punch (p. 26), Party Salsa (p. 26), Orange Cranberry Punch (p. 26), Meatball and Sausage Bites (p. 26), Creamy Deviled Eggs (p. 27), Sunshine Chicken Wings (p. 27) and Baked Crab Dip (p. 27).

LIME SHERBET PUNCH
Jamie Gurney, Odessa, Missouri
(Pictured on page 24)

When I married David in a rural spot, my parents surprised me with a beautiful white carriage to take us to the ceremony. What didn't surprise me was how delicious all the food was since my mother prepared everything, including this pretty pastel punch.

Tip: *Add the ginger ale just before serving to keep the beverage bubbly.*

    2 cartons (1/2 gallon *each*) lime sherbet
    2 cans (46 ounces *each*) pineapple
       juice, chilled
    3 liters ginger ale, chilled

Spoon or scoop sherbet into a large punch bowl. Add pineapple juice and ginger ale. Stir until sherbet is partially melted. Serve immediately. **Yield:** 40 servings (8 quarts).

ORANGE CRANBERRY PUNCH
Brook Hickle, Enumclaw, Washington
(Pictured on page 25)

Our country wedding, held on my parents' farm, was even more wonderful than my husband, Keith, and I had imagined. There were so many memorable touches, including fresh wildflowers and sunflowers, plus great food and beverages like this beautiful citrusy punch. My mom created this simple recipe.

Tip: *Prepare 24 hours ahead to develop the "fruity" flavors. Consider freezing additional cranberry juice in a ring or ice cube trays to chill punch without diluting.*

    4 quarts cranberry juice
    2 cups orange juice
    2 medium oranges, sliced
    2 medium lemons, sliced
    2 medium limes, sliced

In a large glass or plastic container, combine juices and fruit; cover and refrigerate overnight. Serve in pitchers or a large punch bowl. **Yield:** 24 servings (about 4-1/2 quarts).

MEATBALL AND SAUSAGE BITES
Deb Henderson, Maroa, Illinois
(Pictured on page 25)

The Country/Victorian wedding Jim and I planned included a ceremony in front of a hitching post Jim made and two special hula dances (I belong to a Hawaiian dance troupe). A good friend, Linda Allen, prepared this meaty snack, which was a hit.

Tip: *Assemble pans of this appetizer a day ahead, cover and refrigerate. Remove from the refrigerator 30 minutes before baking as directed. Serve from a slow cooker or electric roaster.*

    2 eggs
    1 small onion, finely chopped
    1 cup dry bread crumbs
  1/2 teaspoon garlic salt
  1/2 teaspoon pepper
    2 pounds ground beef
    2 packages (1 pound *each*) miniature
       smoked sausage links
    2 cans (20 ounces *each*) pineapple
       chunks, drained
    1 jar (10 ounces) small stuffed olives,
       drained
    1 cup packed brown sugar
    2 bottles (20 ounces *each*) barbecue
       sauce

In a large bowl, combine the first five ingredients; mix well. Crumble beef over mixture and mix well. Shape into 1-in. balls. Place 1 in. apart on an ungreased 15-in. x 10-in. x 1-in. baking pan. Bake, uncovered, at 350° for 15 minutes or until no longer pink. With a slotted spoon, transfer meatballs to two shallow 3-qt. baking dishes. Add sausages, pineapple and olives to each; toss gently to mix. Combine brown sugar and barbecue sauce; pour half over each casserole. Bake, uncovered, at 350° for 25 minutes or until heated through. **Yield:** about 40 servings.

PARTY SALSA
Toni Swanson, Gull Lake, Saskatchewan
(Pictured on page 25)

My husband's mom, Connie Swanson, prepared a big batch of this pretty and zippy salsa to serve at our wedding reception. It's very special and fresh-tasting. There's no need to peel the tomatoes since they're so finely chopped.

Tip: *Salsa can be refrigerated for up to 5 days.*

  16 medium ripe tomatoes, chopped
    2 large onions, finely chopped
    1 medium green pepper, finely chopped
  1/2 cup minced fresh parsley
    2 to 4 jalapeno peppers, seeded and
       finely chopped*, optional
    2 cans (6 ounces *each*) tomato paste
    3 garlic cloves, minced
    1 can (4 ounces) chopped green chilies

3/4 cup vinegar
2 tablespoons lemon juice
2 teaspoons salt
1 teaspoon pepper
3 tablespoons cornstarch
1/3 cup cold water

In a large Dutch oven or soup kettle, combine the first 12 ingredients; bring to a boil. Reduce heat; simmer, uncovered, for 15 minutes. Combine cornstarch and water until smooth; stir into salsa. Bring to a boil. Cook and stir for 2 minutes; cool. **Yield:** about 2 quarts. ***Editor's Note:*** When cutting or seeding hot peppers, use rubber or plastic gloves to protect your hands. Avoid touching your face.

CREAMY DEVILED EGGS
Barbara Towler, Derby, Ohio
(Pictured on page 25)

These deviled eggs are nicely flavored with a tang of mustard and a spark of sweetness from pickle relish. We served them at the wedding reception of my daughter, Katherine Beth, and Patrick Althouse.

Tip: *For convenience, eggs can be cooked, peeled and chilled up to 2 days before serving.*

3 dozen hard-cooked eggs
1 package (8 ounces) cream cheese, softened
1-1/2 cups mayonnaise *or* salad dressing
1/3 cup sweet pickle relish
1/3 cup Dijon mustard
3/4 teaspoon salt
1/4 teaspoon pepper
Paprika and parsley sprigs

Slice eggs in half lengthwise; remove yolks and set yolks and whites aside. In a mixing bowl, beat cream cheese until smooth. Add the mayonnaise, relish, mustard, salt, pepper and reserved yolks; mix well. Stuff or pipe into egg whites. Garnish with paprika and parsley. Refrigerate several hours before serving. **Yield:** 36 servings.

SUNSHINE CHICKEN WINGS
Ami Miller, Plain City, Ohio
(Pictured on page 24)

Many hands helped make our wedding day perfect. My aunts and cousins prepared the wonderful food. My husband, Jeff, and I and our guests enjoyed these finger-licking-good chicken wings. The zesty sauce was inspired by my uncle, Bill Gingerich.

2 jars (12 ounces *each*) orange marmalade
3 cups ketchup
1 cup packed brown sugar
1 large onion, finely chopped
1/2 cup butter *or* margarine
3 tablespoons chili powder
3 tablespoons vinegar
1 tablespoon Worcestershire sauce
Hot pepper sauce to taste
8 pounds whole chicken wings*
(about 40)

In a large saucepan, combine the first nine ingredients. Bring to a boil. Reduce heat; simmer, uncovered, for 15 minutes. Meanwhile, cut chicken wings into three sections; discard wing tips. Dip wings into sauce and place on two foil-lined 15-in. x 10-in. x 1-in. baking pans. Bake at 350° for 45 minutes, reversing pans once during baking. Serve immediately or cover and refrigerate for up to 2 days before serving. Reheat in the oven, a slow cooker or electric roaster. **Yield:** 15-20 servings. ***Editor's Note:*** 8 pounds of uncooked chicken wing sections may be substituted for the whole chicken wings. Omit the second step of the recipe.

BAKED CRAB DIP
Marie Shelley, Exeter, Missouri
(Pictured on page 24)

In a horseback ceremony, my grandson, Larry Lyons, married his bride, Heidi. This exquisite dip, suggested by Heidi's grandma, Phyllis Kackley, is creamy and delicious. It looks fancy, but is easy to make.

Tip: *The bread can be filled earlier and refrigerated until 1-1/2 hours before serving. Remove from the refrigerator 30 minutes before baking.*

1 package (8 ounces) cream cheese, softened
2 cups (16 ounces) sour cream
2 cans (6 ounces *each*) crabmeat, drained, flaked and cartilage removed *or* 2 cups flaked imitation crabmeat
2 cups (8 ounces) shredded cheddar cheese
4 green onions, thinly sliced
2 round loaves (1 pound *each*) unsliced sourdough *or* Italian bread
Additional sliced green onions, optional
Assorted crackers

In a mixing bowl, beat cream cheese until smooth. Add sour cream; mix well. Fold in crab, cheese and onions. Cut the top third off each loaf of bread; carefully hollow out bottoms, leaving 1-in. shells. Cube removed bread and tops; set aside. Spoon crab mixture into bread bowls. Place on baking sheets. Place reserved bread cubes in a single layer around bread bowls. Bake, uncovered, at 350° for 45-50 minutes or until the dip is heated through. Garnish with green onions if desired. Serve with toasted bread cubes and crackers. **Yield:** 5 cups.

RISING TO THE OCCASION.
From the top are Almond Poppy
Seed Bread (p. 29), Love Knots
(p. 29), plus Butter Hearts (p. 29).

Beautiful Breads

LOVE KNOTS
Beth Estes Johnson
Worcester, Massachusetts
(Pictured on page 28)

My sister, Margo, and I prepared the feast when I wed Richard. These rich, tender rolls were my favorite part of the meal. They absolutely melt in your mouth!

    2 packages (1/4 ounce *each*) active dry yeast
    2 teaspoons plus 1/2 cup sugar, *divided*
1-1/4 cups warm water (110° to 115°)
    3/4 cup warm milk (110° to 115°)
    1/3 cup butter *or* margarine, melted, cooled
    2 eggs, beaten
    2 teaspoons salt
6-1/2 to 7 cups all-purpose flour
    1 egg yolk
    1 tablespoon water
Sesame seeds, optional

In a large mixing bowl, dissolve yeast and 2 teaspoons sugar in water. Add milk, butter, eggs, salt, remaining sugar and 4 cups flour; beat on low for 3 minutes or until smooth. Stir in enough remaining flour to form a soft dough. Turn onto a floured surface; knead until smooth and elastic, about 6-8 minutes. Place in a greased bowl, turning once to grease top. Cover and let rise in a warm place until doubled, about 1 hour. Punch dough down. Divide into four portions. Cover three with plastic wrap. Shape one portion into 12 balls; roll each ball into an 8-in. rope. Tie into a knot; tuck ends under. Pinch to seal. Place 2 in. apart on greased baking sheets. Repeat with remaining three portions. Cover and let rise until doubled, about 25 minutes. Beat egg yolk and water; brush over dough. Sprinkle with sesame seeds if desired. Bake at 375° for 12-15 minutes or until golden brown. **Yield:** 4 dozen.

ALMOND POPPY SEED BREAD
Carole Davis, Keene, New Hampshire
(Pictured on page 28)

We hosted a beautiful wedding for our son, James, and his bride, Margret, and served these lovely loaves to their guests. The recipe came from a dear friend, Judie Tobin.

2-1/4 cups sugar
    1 cup plus 2 tablespoons vegetable oil
    3 eggs
    3 tablespoons poppy seeds
1-1/2 teaspoons lemon juice
1-1/2 teaspoons almond extract
1-1/2 teaspoons vanilla extract
    3 cups all-purpose flour

1-1/2 teaspoons baking powder
    1 teaspoon salt
1-1/2 cups milk
GLAZE:
    3/4 cup confectioners' sugar
    1/4 cup orange juice
    1 teaspoon vanilla extract
    1/2 teaspoon almond extract

In a mixing bowl, combine the first seven ingredients until smooth. Combine flour, baking powder and salt. Add to sugar mixture alternately with milk; beat just until moistened. Pour into two greased 8-in. x 4-in. x 2-in. loaf pans. Bake at 350° for 55-60 minutes or until a toothpick comes out clean. Combine glaze ingredients; brush over warm loaves. Cool 10 minutes before removing from pans to wire racks. **Yield:** 2 loaves.

GOLDEN CHEESE YEAST BREAD
Toni Swanson, Gull Lake, Saskatchewan

My husband, Mark, and I wanted a casual wedding and decided on a cold plate buffet supper. This fun cheesy bread baked by my mom was a special addition.

    6 to 7 cups all-purpose flour
    2 cups (8 ounces) shredded cheddar cheese
    3 tablespoons sugar
    2 packages (1/4 ounce *each*) active dry yeast
    2 teaspoons salt
    2 cups warm milk (120° to 130°)
    1 egg

In a large mixing bowl, combine 3 cups flour, cheese, sugar, yeast and salt. Add milk and egg; beat on low speed until smooth. Stir in enough remaining flour to form a soft dough. Turn onto a floured surface; knead until smooth and elastic, about 6-8 minutes. Place in a greased bowl, turning once to grease top. Cover and let rise in a warm place until doubled, about 1 hour. Punch dough down. Divide in half and shape into two loaves. Place in two greased 9-in. x 5-in. x 3-in. loaf pans. Cover and let rise until doubled, about 45 minutes. Bake at 375° for 25-30 minutes or until golden brown. Remove from pans to cool on wire racks. **Yield:** 2 loaves.

BUTTER HEARTS
(Pictured on page 28)

1/2 cup cold butter (no substitutes)

Cut butter into 16 slices, about 1/4 in. thick. Place on a baking sheet lined with waxed paper. Freeze for 5-10 minutes or until firm. Cut each slice using a 1-1/2-in. heart-shaped cookie cutter. **Yield:** 16 hearts.

MOUTH-WATERING MAIN DISHES like these ensure that even those with big appetites walk away from the wedding buffet satisfied! Clockwise from center: Teriyaki Chicken (p. 32), Roast Beef with Onion Au Jus (p. 32), 1-2-3 Barbecued Sausage (p. 32), Sweet 'n' Moist Ham (p. 33) and Flavorful Beef Brisket (p. 32).

1-2-3 BARBECUED SAUSAGE
Clara Johnson, Eldorado, Ohio
(Pictured on page 31)

When my husband, Joe, and I hosted our Western wedding, good friend Kay Skiles prepared a tempting buffet meal that included this tangy easy-to-fix sausage.

> **6 pounds fully cooked smoked sausage, cut into 2-inch pieces**
> **2 bottles (18 ounces *each*) barbecue sauce**
> **2 cups packed brown sugar**

Divide sausages between two ungreased 13-in. x 9-in. x 2-in. baking dishes. Combine barbecue sauce and brown sugar; pour over sausages and toss to coat. Bake, uncovered, at 350° for 35-40 minutes or until sauce is thickened, stirring once. **Yield:** about 24 servings.

FLAVORFUL BEEF BRISKET
Jamie Gurney, Odessa, Missouri
(Pictured on page 30)

A memorable part of my wedding day was the supper my mom prepared. This moist fork-tender brisket is a popular entree hearty appetites appreciate.

> **Tip:** *Refrigerating the beef overnight makes it possible to slice it very thinly.*

> **1 beef brisket* (about 5 pounds)**
> **2 tablespoons vegetable oil**
> **1 medium onion, sliced**
> Salt and pepper to taste
> **1 cup water**
> **1 bottle (18 ounces) barbecue sauce**

In a Dutch oven, brown beef in oil on both sides over medium-high heat; drain. Top with onion, salt and pepper. Add water; cover and bake at 325° for 2-1/2 hours or until tender. Remove beef; refrigerate overnight. Discard onion and cooking liquid. Slice meat 1/4 in. thick; place in a roasting pan. Add barbecue sauce. Cover and bake at 325° for 30-45 minutes or until heated through. **Yield:** 16-18 servings. ***Editor's Note:** This is a fresh beef brisket, not corned beef.

ROAST BEEF WITH ONION AU JUS
Dawn Hembd, Whitehall, Wisconsin
(Pictured on page 31)

My brother, Rick, raised the beef for our wedding. My cousin, Jackie Reader, turned 60 pounds of it into this delicious entree, which can also be served on rolls.

> **Tip:** *Reheat in an electric roaster or slow cooker.*

> **2 boneless eye of round *or* rump roasts (about 3 pounds *each*)**
> **8 garlic cloves, peeled**
> **1/4 cup vegetable oil**
> **1 envelope onion soup mix**
> **2 cups water**
> Additional water *or* beef broth
> **1 envelope au jus gravy mix**

With a sharp knife, make four slits in the top of each roast and insert garlic cloves into slits. In a Dutch oven over medium-high heat, brown roasts on all sides in oil; drain. Rub soup mix over meat. Add water to the pan; cover and bake at 325° for 2-1/2 to 3 hours or until tender. Remove meat from cooking liquid; cool meat. Cover and refrigerate overnight. Skim fat from cooking liquid; refrigerate in a covered container. Slice beef 1/4 in. thick; set aside. Measure cooking liquid. If needed, add enough water or beef broth to measure 3 cups. In a Dutch oven, combine au jus mix and reserved cooking liquid until smooth. Cook and stir over medium heat until mixture comes to a boil. Reduce heat; add sliced beef and reheat on low for 15-20 minutes. **Yield:** 18-20 servings.

TERIYAKI CHICKEN
Edna Luce, Kearney, Nebraska
(Pictured on page 30)

When my granddaughter, Alicia Fie, married James Reeves, our family served this flavorful chicken over rice. It requires very little last-minute fuss.

> **Tip:** *Keep chicken hot in an electric roaster set on low. A bit of beef broth will keep the meat moist.*

> **3/4 cup vegetable oil**
> **3/4 cup soy sauce**
> **1/3 cup chili sauce**
> **3 tablespoons sesame seeds**
> **3 tablespoons vinegar**
> **6 garlic cloves, minced**
> **1-1/2 teaspoons sugar**
> **3/4 teaspoon ground ginger**
> **3/4 teaspoon pepper**
> **24 boneless skinless chicken breast halves (about 6 ounces *each*)**
> Toasted sesame seeds

In a bowl, combine the first nine ingredients; pour 3/4 cup marinade into each of three large resealable plastic bags. Add eight chicken breasts to each bag; seal bags and turn to coat. Refrigerate for 6 hours or overnight, turning once. Discard marinade. Transfer to two greased 15-in. x 10-in. x 1-

in. baking pans. Bake, uncovered, at 350° for 20-25 minutes or until chicken juices run clear, turning once. To grill, cook, uncovered, over medium-hot heat for 10-14 minutes or until chicken juices run clear, turning once. Sprinkle with sesame seeds before serving. **Yield:** 24 servings.

SWEET 'N' MOIST HAM
Dawn Hembd, Whitehall, Wisconsin
(Pictured on page 30)

We served 75 pounds of ham fixed this way. It could not be simpler, and it's moist and delightfully sweet.

1 sliced boneless fully cooked ham
   (about 6 pounds), tied
1 can (12 ounces) lemon-lime soda

Place ham on a rack in a shallow roasting pan. Pour soda over ham. Cover and bake at 325° for 2 hours or until a meat thermometer reads 140° and ham is heated through. **Yield:** 18-20 servings.

ITALIAN PASTA SAUCE
Judy Braun, Juneau, Wisconsin

As a special part of their wedding buffet, my daughter Kris' husband, Jim Oliva, fixed a big batch of this thick flavorful pasta sauce. The recipe was brought by his grandmother from Italy 80 years ago.

4 pounds ground beef
1 pound bulk Italian sausage
1 large onion, finely chopped
3 celery ribs, finely chopped
4 garlic cloves, minced
2 tablespoons olive *or* vegetable oil
3 cans (28 ounces *each*) crushed
   tomatoes in puree
3 cans (6 ounces *each*) tomato paste
3 cups chicken *or* beef broth
1 pound fresh mushrooms, sliced
3/4 cup minced fresh parsley
1 tablespoon sugar
2 to 3 teaspoons salt
1/2 teaspoon pepper
1/2 teaspoon ground allspice, optional
Hot cooked pasta

In a Dutch oven or soup kettle, cook beef in two batches over medium heat until no longer pink; drain and set aside. Cook sausage over medium heat until no longer pink; drain and set aside. In the same pan, saute onion, celery and garlic in oil until vegetables are tender. Return the beef and sausage to the pan. Add the remaining ingredients and bring to a boil. Reduce heat; cover and simmer for 2-3 hours or until desired thickness is reached, stirring occasionally. Serve over pasta. **Yield:** 20 servings.

CHICKEN TETRAZZINI
Andrea Hutchison, Canton, Oklahoma

Our son, Newley, and our daughter, Kasse, both were married within a month and a half. We served this delicious and comforting casserole to their guests. It's a recipe my mother-in-law relied on for 25 years.

1 large green pepper, chopped
1 medium onion, chopped
1/2 cup butter *or* margarine
2/3 cup all-purpose flour
1/2 teaspoon garlic powder
1/4 teaspoon pepper
4 cups milk
1 can (10-3/4 ounces) condensed cream
   of chicken soup, undiluted
10 slices process sharp cheddar cheese,
   cubed
10 slices process American cheese, cubed
5 cups cubed cooked chicken
1 package (16 ounces) frozen peas
1 jar (4 ounces) diced pimientos, drained
1 package (1 pound) spaghetti, cooked,
   rinsed and drained
1/4 cup slivered almonds, optional
1/4 cup minced fresh parsley

In a Dutch oven, saute green pepper and onion in butter until crisp-tender. Stir in flour, garlic powder and pepper until blended. Gradually add milk. Bring to a boil. Cook and stir for 2 minutes or until thickened. Stir in soup, cheeses and chicken; cook and stir until cheese is melted. Stir in peas, pimientos and spaghetti. Transfer to two greased 13-in. x 9-in. x 2-in. baking dishes. Top with almonds if desired. Bake, uncovered, at 350° for 20-30 minutes or until heated through. Garnish with parsley. **Yield:** 20-24 servings.

ORANGE BARBECUE SAUCE
Heidi Rhodes, Edgerton, Ohio

When Jerry and I got married, I worked with a friend to choose food that our farmer friends with big appetites would like. The highlight was a pig roast topped with this tangy barbecue sauce.

4 cups ketchup
1 cup prepared mustard
1 cup orange juice
1 large onion, finely chopped
1/2 cup packed brown sugar
4 teaspoons liquid smoke, optional
4 garlic cloves, minced
2 teaspoons pepper

In a large saucepan, combine all ingredients; bring to a boil. Reduce heat; simmer, uncovered, for 30 minutes. May be refrigerated for up to 1 week. Use as a basting or dipping sauce for pork, poultry or beef. **Yield:** 4 cups.

HOMESPUN HOT SIDE DISHES like the terrific ones here are the perfect way to round out a country wedding meal! From the top: Garlic Roasted Potatoes (p. 35), Hearty Bean Side Dish (p. 35) and Summer Squash Casserole (p. 35).

Hearty Hot Side Dishes

GARLIC ROASTED POTATOES
Heidi Rhodes, Edgerton, Ohio
(Pictured on page 34)

A good friend provided the food for the one-of-a-kind Western-style wedding Jerry and I planned. These potatoes are scrumptious and easy to fix since there's no need to peel them.

Tip: *If you cut the potatoes early in the day, cover with cold water to keep from darkening. Drain just before combining with butter and seasonings.*

> 9 pounds small red potatoes, cut into
>   1-1/2-inch wedges
> 1-1/4 cups butter *or* margarine, melted
> 6 garlic cloves, minced
> 1 tablespoon seasoned salt
> 1 tablespoon pepper
> 1 tablespoon paprika
> 1/3 cup minced fresh parsley

Place potatoes in a large greased roasting pan. Combine butter, garlic, salt, pepper and paprika. Drizzle over potatoes; toss to coat. Bake at 375° for 30-35 minutes or until tender, stirring several times. Sprinkle with parsley. **Yield:** 26-30 servings.

HEARTY BEAN SIDE DISH
Tina Roberts, Wellington, Ohio
(Pictured on page 34)

In a small, simple ceremony on the farm, my mother, Betty, married Ron Kreiling. I prepared this hearty down-home dish to share.

Tip: *Refrigerate up to 2 days; reheat to serve. Keep warm in a slow cooker or electric roaster.*

> 1 pound fully cooked smoked sausage
>   links, sliced
> 1 can (28 ounces) pork and beans,
>   undrained
> 1 can (16 ounces) kidney beans, rinsed
>   and drained
> 1 can (15-1/2 ounces) chili beans in chili
>   sauce, undrained
> 1 can (15 ounces) lima beans, drained
> 1 can (14-1/2 ounces) cut wax beans,
>   drained
> 1 can (14-1/2 ounces) cut green beans,
>   drained
> 1 can (10-3/4 ounces) condensed tomato
>   soup, undiluted
> 1 can (6 ounces) tomato paste
> 1/2 cup packed brown sugar
> 1/2 cup barbecue sauce

In a Dutch oven or soup kettle, combine all ingredients. Bring to a boil. Reduce heat; cover and simmer for 20 minutes or until heated through. **Yield:** 16-20 servings. **Editor's Note:** 1 pound cooked and drained ground beef may be substituted for the sausage.

SUMMER SQUASH CASSEROLE
Carole Davis, Keene, New Hampshire
(Pictured on page 34)

This fresh-tasting side dish is excellent with any meat. It was a popular part of the meal served at the August wedding of our son James and his bride, Margret.

Tip: *Assemble casserole, cover and refrigerate. Remove from the refrigerator 30 minutes before baking.*

> 18 cups sliced zucchini *or* yellow summer
>   squash (about 6 pounds)
> 6 medium carrots, shredded
> 3 medium onions, chopped
> 1-1/2 cups butter *or* margarine, *divided*
> 3 cans (10-3/4-ounces *each*) condensed
>   cream of chicken soup, undiluted
> 3 cups (24 ounces) sour cream
> 3 packages (8 ounces *each*) crushed
>   stuffing mix

In a Dutch oven, saute squash, carrots and onions in 6 tablespoons butter until tender; remove from the heat. Stir in soup and sour cream. Melt the remaining butter; add to stuffing mix. Gently stir into the squash mixture. Transfer to two greased 13-in. x 9-in. x 2-in. baking dishes. Bake, uncovered, at 350° for 35-40 minutes or until stuffing is heated through. **Yield:** 26-30 servings.

EASY PORK 'N' BEANS
Marilyn Niemeyer, Doon, Iowa

Friends prepared the food, including these simple yet delicious baked beans, when our daughter, Briana, married Jerad Van Der Zwaag. Chili powder enhances canned beans for a rich crowd-pleasing dish.

> 2 cans (55 ounces *each*) pork and beans
> 2 large onions, chopped
> 10 bacon strips, cooked and crumbled
> 1-1/4 cups packed brown sugar
> 1/3 cup vinegar
> 1/3 cup ketchup
> 5 teaspoons chili powder
> 1 tablespoon ground mustard

In a Dutch oven, combine all ingredients; bring to a boil over medium-high heat. Reduce heat; cover and simmer for 1 hour or until heated through. **Yield:** 16-20 servings.

SKILLET ZUCCHINI
Linda Fabian, Wheatland, Wyoming

A dear aunt shared this dish and recipe for our potluck wedding dinner. It's a savory combination of sausage, onions, peppers and zucchini in a tomato-based sauce—delicious!

Tip: *This side item can be prepared the day before serving. Simply cook the zucchini for 3-4 minutes, then cover and refrigerate the mixture overnight. Reheat in a large kettle before serving.*

- 1 pound fully cooked kielbasa *or* Polish sausage links, cut into 1/4-inch slices
- 1/4 cup vegetable oil
- 2 medium green peppers, chopped
- 2 cups sliced celery
- 1 large onion, chopped
- 2 garlic cloves, minced
- 8 to 10 medium zucchini, cut into 1/4-inch slices
- 2 cans (28 ounces *each*) diced tomatoes, undrained
- 2 teaspoons dried oregano
- 2 teaspoons salt
- 1 teaspoon pepper

In a Dutch oven, cook sausage in oil over medium heat until browned. Add the peppers, celery, onion and garlic; saute for 5 minutes or until vegetables are crisp-tender. Stir in the zucchini, tomatoes, oregano, salt and pepper. Bring to a boil. Reduce heat; cover and simmer for 6-8 minutes or until zucchini is tender. **Yield:** 24-26 servings.

SPOON BREAD CORN CASSEROLE
Linda Fabian, Wheatland, Wyoming

To keep our wedding simple and fun, Joe and I asked our guests to bring their favorite covered dish and a copy of the recipe (I wanted to put together a wedding cookbook later). We ended up with an outstanding buffet, including this delightful down-home casserole. The recipe came from Erma Thoeming.

Tip: *Bake the day before, cool, cover and refrigerate. The next day, reheat at 350°, uncovered, for 15 to 20 minutes.*

- 2 cups (16 ounces) sour cream
- 1 cup butter *or* margarine, melted and cooled
- 2 packages (8-1/2 ounces *each*) corn bread/muffin mix
- 2 cans (15-1/4 ounces *each*) whole kernel corn, drained
- 2 cans (14-3/4 ounces *each*) cream-style corn
- 1/4 cup diced pimientos
- 1/8 teaspoon salt
- 1/8 teaspoon pepper
- 1/8 teaspoon cayenne pepper

In a large bowl, combine sour cream and butter; stir in muffin mixes. Fold in the remaining ingredients. Transfer to two greased 8-in. square baking dishes. Bake, uncovered, at 350° for 55-60 minutes or until a knife inserted near center comes out clean. Serve warm. **Yield:** about 32 servings.

OLD-FASHIONED BAKED BEANS
Alvinia King, Rudolph, Wisconsin

These traditional baked beans have a nice blend of flavors and a thick pleasant sauce. They were a hit at our son's wedding.

Tip: *If several batches are needed, cook and serve in an electric roaster for convenience.*

- 2 pounds dry navy beans
- 4 quarts water
- 2 large onions, chopped
- 1/2 pound bacon *or* salt pork, cut into 1/2-inch pieces
- 1-1/2 cups ketchup
- 1/2 cup molasses
- 1/2 cup packed brown sugar
- 2 tablespoons prepared mustard
- 1 tablespoon salt

Place beans in a Dutch oven or soup kettle; add water to cover by 2 in. Bring to a boil; boil for 2 minutes. Remove from the heat; cover and let stand 1 hour. Drain and rinse beans, discarding liquid. Return beans to Dutch oven; add 4 qts. water. Bring to a boil. Reduce heat; cover and simmer for 1 hour or until the beans are almost tender. Drain and reserve liquid. Combine beans with the remaining ingredients. Transfer to two ungreased 2-1/2-qt. baking dishes or bean pots. Add 1-1/2 cups reserved cooking liquid to each casserole; stir to combine. Cover and bake at 300° for 3 hours or until beans are tender and reach desired consistency, stirring every 30 minutes. Add reserved cooking liquid during baking as needed. **Yield:** 16-18 servings.

MAKE-AHEAD SCALLOPED POTATOES
Linda Cox, Embarrass, Minnesota

After our memorable lakeside ceremony, guests gathered with Creighton and me at a nearby hall for our reception. A dear friend, Sharon Kramer, fixed good home-style food. Her tempting menu included these delicious potatoes. They're special, but made with convenient canned soup.

- 8 pounds potatoes, peeled and thinly sliced
- 2 large onions, thinly sliced
- 1/3 cup all-purpose flour

2 cans (10-3/4 ounces *each*) condensed
  cream of chicken soup, undiluted
2-2/3 cups milk
Salt and pepper to taste
2 cups (8 ounces) shredded cheddar
  cheese

In two greased 13-in. x 9-in. x 2-in. baking dishes, layer potatoes and onions. Combine the flour,
soup and milk until blended; pour over each baking dish. Season with salt and pepper. Cover and
bake at 325° for 1-1/4 to 1-1/2 hours or until
potatoes are tender. Uncover; cool for 30 minutes. Cover and refrigerate overnight. Remove
from refrigerator 30 minutes before reheating.
Bake at 325° for 30-40 minutes. Uncover and
sprinkle with cheese; bake 5 minutes longer or until cheese is melted. **Yield:** about 20 servings.

RICH POTATO CASSEROLE
Pat Coffee, Kingston, Washington
(Pictured below)

*I got the recipe for these irresistible potatoes from a
friend in my country line-dance club several years
ago. It's a favorite at every potluck I've taken it to.
So when I married Cliff on our farm, this saucy dish
was automatically part of the wedding menu.*

Tip: *Assemble casserole; cover and refrigerate. Remove from the refrigerator 30 minutes before baking.*

2 packages (30 ounces *each*) country-
  style shredded hash browns, thawed

3/4 cup butter *or* margarine, melted,
  divided
4 cups (32 ounces) sour cream
2 cans (10-3/4 ounces *each*) condensed
  cream of chicken soup, undiluted
1 bunch green onions, sliced
4 cups (16 ounces) shredded cheddar
  cheese
1 teaspoon salt
1/4 teaspoon pepper
1-1/2 cups cornflakes, crushed

In a large bowl, combine the potatoes, 1/2 cup butter, sour cream, soup, onions, cheese, salt and
pepper. Transfer to two greased shallow 3-qt. baking dishes. Combine cornflakes and remaining
butter; sprinkle evenly over tops. Bake, uncovered,
at 350° for 55-60 minutes or until bubbly. **Yield:**
26-30 servings.

HOMEMADE NOODLES
Alvinia King, Rudolph, Wisconsin

*When our son Conrad married Erin on our dairy
farm, family and friends helped me prepare food for
400. To go with grilled pork and chicken, we fixed an
array of side dishes, including these wonderful noodles. At this Polish wedding, we wanted to be sure no
one went home hungry.*

Tip: *Noodles will stay warm and hold a long
time in a slow cooker or electric roaster.*

6 to 7 cups all-purpose flour
1-1/2 teaspoons salt
6 eggs, beaten
1 cup water
1 tablespoon vegetable oil
Melted butter and minced fresh parsley,
  optional

In a large bowl, combine 6 cups flour and salt.
Make a well in the center; add eggs and water. Mix
with a wooden spoon until well combined. Gather into a ball; knead on a well-floured surface until smooth, about 10 minutes. If necessary, add remaining flour to keep dough from sticking to work
surface or hands. Cover with a towel; let stand 10
minutes. Divide dough into eight portions. On a
lightly floured surface, roll each portion into a
1/16-in.-thick square. Let stand, uncovered, for 10
minutes. Roll up, jelly-roll style. Using a sharp
knife, cut into 1/4-in. slices. Unroll noodles and
dry in a single layer on paper towels for 1 hour before cooking. To cook, bring salted water to a rapid
boil. Add noodles and oil to boiling water; cook for
2 minutes or until tender but not soft. Drain; toss
with butter and parsley if desired. **Yield:** 24 servings. **Editor's Note:** Uncooked noodles may be
stored in the refrigerator for 2-3 days or frozen for
up to 1 month.

SUPER SAVORY AND SWEET SALADS like these add a refreshing spark to special spreads honoring the bride and groom. Clockwise from top left: Marinated Vegetable Bean Salad (p. 40), Golden Potato Salad (p. 41), Colorful Barley Salad (p. 40), Frosted Strawberry Salad (p. 41), Antipasto Salad (p. 40) and Copper Carrot Salad (p. 40).

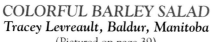

COLORFUL BARLEY SALAD
Tracey Levreault, Baldur, Manitoba
(Pictured on page 39)

Chili powder and cumin give this distinctive barley salad a subtle Tex-Mex flavor. It's a super make-ahead side dish. Folks commented on how hearty and tasty it was when we served it at our wedding barbecue.

    3 cans (10-1/2 ounces *each*) condensed
       chicken broth, undiluted
    4 cups water
    3 cups medium pearl barley
    1 cup vegetable oil
    1/3 cup vinegar
    3 garlic cloves, minced
    1-1/2 teaspoons chili powder
    1-1/2 teaspoons ground cumin
    6 large tomatoes, seeded and chopped
    1 package (16 ounces) frozen corn
    1 bunch green onions, sliced
    1 cup minced fresh parsley

In a large soup kettle or Dutch oven, bring chicken broth and water to a boil. Add barley; reduce the heat. Cover and simmer for 35-40 minutes or until barley is tender. Cool slightly. Combine the oil, vinegar, garlic, chili powder and cumin; pour over barley and toss well. Gently stir in the remaining ingredients. Transfer to a serving bowl; cover and refrigerate overnight. **Yield:** 24 servings.

MARINATED VEGETABLE BEAN SALAD
Kendra Waterbury, E. Thetford, Vermont
(Pictured on page 38)

Canned beans make this colorful salad hearty...and bottled Italian dressing is an easy and tasty topper.

    2 cans (16 ounces *each*) kidney beans,
       rinsed and drained
    2 cans (14-1/2 ounces *each*) cut green
       beans, drained
    2 cans (14-1/2 ounces *each*) wax beans,
       drained
    1 jar (10 ounces) small stuffed olives,
       drained
    6 cups broccoli florets, finely chopped
       (about 2 pounds)
    2 medium green peppers, chopped
    2 medium sweet red peppers, chopped
    1 medium red onion, chopped
    1 teaspoon dried basil
    1/2 teaspoon garlic salt
    1 bottle (16 ounces) Italian salad
       dressing

In a large salad bowl, combine the first 10 ingredients. Pour dressing over salad; toss to coat. Cover and refrigerate overnight. Stir before serving. **Yield:** about 20 servings.

COPPER CARROT SALAD
Dianna Badgett, St. Maries, Idaho
(Pictured on page 38)

This colorful quick-to-fix salad has been made by my family for many years. My mom, Jean Hamm, shared the recipe so I could have it in my wedding dinner.

    5 pounds carrots, cut into 1/4-inch slices
    2 medium green peppers, chopped
    1 large onion, chopped
    2 cans (10-3/4 ounces *each*) condensed
       tomato soup, undiluted
    1-1/2 cups sugar
    1-1/2 cups vinegar
    1 cup vegetable oil
    6 teaspoons Italian seasoning
    2 teaspoons ground mustard
    2 teaspoons curry powder
    2 teaspoons Worcestershire sauce
    1/2 teaspoon salt
    1/2 teaspoon pepper

Place carrots in a large kettle or Dutch oven. Add 1 in. of water. Bring to a boil. Reduce heat; cover and simmer for 15-20 minutes or until tender. Rinse in cold water and drain. In a large bowl, combine green peppers, onion and carrots; set aside. In a large saucepan, combine the remaining ingredients; cook over medium heat until sugar is dissolved. Cool for 10 minutes. Pour over carrot mixture. Cover and refrigerate for 24 hours. Serve with a slotted spoon. **Yield:** 16 servings.

ANTIPASTO SALAD
Kendra Waterbury, E. Thetford, Vermont
(Pictured on page 38)

I always told my sister, Karen, I'd marry a cowboy...and I did! Patrick and I had a festive farm-style wedding. My mother prepared all the side dishes, including this tongue-tingling salad.

Tip: The dressing can be made up to a week ahead and refrigerated until salad is ready to assemble.

    2 packages (16 ounces *each*) spiral pasta
    2 cans (15 ounces *each*) garbanzo beans
       or chickpeas, rinsed and drained
    2 packages (3-1/2 ounces *each*) sliced
       pepperoni, halved

2 cans (2-1/4 ounces *each*) sliced ripe
   olives, drained
3 cups sliced fresh mushrooms
2 medium sweet red peppers, chopped
2 medium green peppers, chopped

DRESSING:

2 cups olive *or* vegetable oil
1-1/3 cups lemon juice
4 garlic cloves, minced
1/4 cup minced fresh basil *or* 4 teaspoons
   dried basil
4 teaspoons salt
1 tablespoon minced fresh oregano *or* 1
   teaspoon dried oregano
1/2 teaspoon pepper
1/4 teaspoon cayenne pepper

Cook pasta according to package directions; rinse in cold water and drain. In a large salad bowl, combine the pasta, beans, pepperoni, olives, mushrooms and peppers. In a 1-qt. jar with a tight-fitting lid, combine the dressing ingredients; shake well. Pour over pasta mixture; toss to coat. Cover and refrigerate for 6 hours or overnight. Just before serving, stir to coat. **Yield:** 24 servings.

FROSTED STRAWBERRY SALAD
Barbara Towler, Derby, Ohio
(Pictured on page 39)

My daughter, Katherine Beth, has requested that her grandmother, Thelma Bell, make this sweet rich gelatin salad with its fluffy topping for every family get-together. So when she and Patrick Althouse planned their nuptials, this delightful salad was part of the bountiful potluck buffet.

2 packages (6 ounces *each*) strawberry
   gelatin
3 cups boiling water
2 packages (10 ounces *each*) frozen
   sweetened sliced strawberries, thawed
1 can (20 ounces) crushed pineapple,
   undrained
1 cup chopped pecans
1/2 cup chopped maraschino cherries

TOPPING:

1 package (8 ounces) cream cheese,
   softened
1 jar (7 ounces) marshmallow creme
1 carton (8 ounces) frozen whipped
   topping, thawed
Fresh strawberries and mint

In a large bowl, dissolve gelatin in boiling water. Stir in strawberries and pineapple. Refrigerate until partially set. Stir in pecans and cherries; transfer to a 13-in. x 9-in. x 2-in. dish. Chill until firm, about 2 hours. For topping, beat cream cheese and marshmallow creme just until combined; fold in whipped topping. Spread over salad. Refrigerate for several hours or overnight. Cut into squares. Garnish with strawberries and mint. **Yield:** 16-20 servings.

GOLDEN POTATO SALAD
Lanore Rasmussen, Twin Falls, Idaho
(Pictured on page 38)

The recipe for this zippy potato salad has been in our family five generations. We always have it at outdoor suppers. Mustard gives the salad appealing color.

Tip: Cook the potatoes a day ahead. Chill in the refrigerator overnight for easy handling.

5 pounds potatoes, cooked, peeled and
   cubed
6 hard-cooked eggs, chopped
1 cup diced celery
1 cup diced dill pickles
1/2 cup sliced green onions
1/2 cup shredded carrot
1/4 cup minced fresh parsley
1 can (6 ounces) pitted small ripe olives,
   drained
2 cups mayonnaise
1/4 cup prepared mustard
1 teaspoon prepared horseradish
1 garlic clove, minced
Salt and pepper to taste

In a large bowl, combine the first eight ingredients. Combine the mayonnaise, mustard, horseradish, garlic, salt and pepper. Pour over potato mixture; toss gently to coat. Cover and refrigerate for several hours or overnight. **Yield:** 20 servings.

HEARTY MACARONI SALAD
Toni Swanson, Gull Lake, Saskatchewan

My grandmother, Marguerite Lemire, makes this old-fashioned side dish for every family function. This hearty chilled salad has classic ingredients plus a bit of vinegar to give it zing.

1 package (16 ounces) elbow macaroni
2 cups (16 ounces) cubed fully cooked
   ham
1 block (8 ounces) cheddar cheese, diced
2 cups mayonnaise *or* salad dressing
1 package (10 ounces) frozen peas,
   thawed
4 green onions, thinly sliced
2 tablespoons vinegar
1/2 teaspoon pepper

Cook macaroni according to package directions; rinse in cold water and drain. Refrigerate until chilled. In a large bowl, combine the remaining ingredients; stir in macaroni. Cover and refrigerate for several hours or overnight. **Yield:** 16 servings.

Scrumptious Sweets

FRESH BERRY PIE
Barbara Rossi, Walla Walla, Washington
(Pictured on page 43)

Our family and friends helped make the wedding of our daughter, Hannah, to Robert Aguilera a truly beautiful day. From the music…to the flowers…to the luncheon buffet, folks pitched in. This pie was one of the many wonderful desserts.

Tip: Bake pastry shells several days ahead if desired. Store cooled shells in air-tight containers.

> 1-1/2 cups sugar
> 1/4 cup cornstarch
> Pinch salt
> 1-1/2 cups cold water
>   1 package (3 ounces) strawberry *or* raspberry gelatin
>   1 quart fresh strawberries *or* raspberries
>   1 pastry shell (9 inches), baked
> Whipped cream and fresh mint, optional

In a saucepan, combine the sugar, cornstarch, salt and water until smooth; bring to a boil over medium-high heat. Cook and stir for 2 minutes. Remove from the heat; stir in dry gelatin until dissolved. Cool until mixture begins to partially set. Remove stems from strawberries. Arrange berries, tip end up, in pastry shell; spoon gelatin mixture over fruit. Refrigerate until set, about 2 hours. Garnish with whipped cream and mint if desired. **Yield:** 6-8 servings.

BRAIDED SWEETHEART COOKIES
Rhonda Berstad, Melfort, Saskatchewan
(Pictured on page 43)

Everyone had a "hay day" when our daughter, Naomi, married Philip Shellenberg. Naomi's grandma, Lilly Person, who has made these tender cookies for 48 years, fixed them in the shape of hearts for the wedding. They got gobbled up in a "heartbeat".

Tip: Fix cookies ahead and freeze until serving.

>   1 cup butter (no substitutes), softened
> 1-1/2 cups confectioners' sugar
>   1 egg
>   1/2 teaspoon vanilla extract
> 2-1/4 cups all-purpose flour
>   1/2 teaspoon baking powder
>   1/2 teaspoon salt
>   6 to 8 drops red food coloring

In a mixing bowl, cream butter and sugar. Beat in egg and vanilla. Combine the flour, baking powder and salt; gradually add to creamed mixture. Divide dough in half; tint one portion pink, leaving the remaining portion white. Wrap each portion in plastic wrap; refrigerate for 4 hours or overnight. For each cookie, shape a 1-in. ball of each color into an 8-in. rope. Place a pink and white rope side-by-side; press together gently and twist. Place 2 in. apart on ungreased baking sheets; shape into a heart and pinch ends to seal. Bake at 350° for 8-11 minutes or until edges are lightly browned. Cool on wire racks. **Yield:** 2 dozen. **Editor's Note:** If cookies spread during baking, place the baking sheets with shaped dough in the freezer for 10 minutes, then bake for 11-12 minutes.

CHOCOLATE CHEESE PIE
Lorra Rhyner, Poynette, Wisconsin
(Pictured on page 43)

Mark and I were married in a casual outdoor ceremony. Our "wedding cake" consisted of 30 delicious cheesecakes, including this easy but special one.

Tip: You can skip the chocolate step and top the plain cheesecake with cherry or blueberry pie filling instead.

>   3 cups graham cracker crumbs (about 48 squares)
>   1/2 cup sugar
>   2/3 cup butter *or* margarine, melted
> FILLING:
>   3 packages (8 ounces *each*) cream cheese, softened
>   1 cup sugar
>   5 eggs
>   1 tablespoon vanilla extract
>   1 package (4 ounces) German sweet chocolate, melted and cooled

In a bowl, combine the first three ingredients. Divide in half and press onto the bottoms and up the sides of two ungreased 9-in. pie plates. Refrigerate while preparing filling. In a large mixing bowl, beat cream cheese on medium speed until fluffy. Gradually add sugar, beating until smooth. Add eggs, one at a time, beating just until blended. Beat in vanilla. Remove 1-1/2 cups cheese mixture to a small bowl; fold in melted chocolate. Divide remaining cream cheese mixture between pie crusts. To make the chain of hearts on each pie, drop teaspoonfuls of chocolate filling, forming 8 drops equally spaced around outside edges and 4 drops in center. Starting in the center of one outer drop, run a knife through the center of each to connect the drops and form a circle of hearts. Repeat with center drops. Bake at 350° for 40-45 minutes or until center is almost set. Cool on wire racks for 1 hour. Refrigerate for at least 6 hours or overnight. **Yield:** 2 pies (8 servings each).

TEMPTING TREATS like these make a mealtime finale grand enough to match the big day. From the top: Fresh Berry Pie (p. 42), Chocolate Cheese Pie (p. 42), Braided Sweetheart Cookies (p. 42) and Wedding Swan Cream Puffs (p. 44).

WEDDING SWAN CREAM PUFFS
Carole Davis, Keene, New Hampshire
(Pictured on page 43)

Grandpa's farm was the setting for our serviceman son's wedding to his German bride. The reception included special touches like these impressive elegant pastries. They look beautiful and taste marvelous.

Tip: *Pudding makes these swans a last-minute dessert. If you want to refrigerate the cream puffs several hours before serving, consider filling with sweetened whipped cream instead.*

    1 cup water
    1/2 cup butter (no substitutes)
    1/4 teaspoon salt
    1 cup all-purpose flour
    4 eggs
Pastry bag *or* heavy-duty resealable plastic bag
#7 round pastry tip
    2 packages (3.4 ounces *each*) instant
        vanilla pudding mix
    2 tablespoons seedless raspberry jam,
        optional
Confectioners' sugar

In a heavy saucepan, bring water, butter and salt to a boil over medium heat. Add flour all at once; stir until a smooth ball forms. Remove from the heat; let stand 5 minutes. Add eggs, one at a time, beating well after each addition. Beat until smooth and shiny. Cut a small hole in the corner of pastry or plastic bag; insert tip. On a greased baking sheet, pipe thirty-six 2-in.-long "S" shapes for the swan necks, making a small dollop at the end of each for the head. Bake at 400° for 5-8 minutes or until golden brown. Remove to wire racks to cool. For the swan bodies, drop remaining batter by 36 level tablespoonfuls 2 in. apart onto greased baking sheets. With a small icing knife or spatula, shape batter into 2-in. x 1-1/2-in. teardrops. Bake at 400° for 30-35 minutes or until golden brown. Cool on wire racks. Meanwhile, prepare pudding according to package directions for pie filling; chill. Just before serving, cut off top third of swan bodies; set tops aside. Remove any soft dough inside. Spoon filling into bottoms of puffs. Top each with a small amount of jam if desired. Cut reserved tops in half lengthwise to form wings; set wings in filling. Place necks in filling. Dust with confectioners' sugar; serve immediately. **Yield:** 3 dozen.

BRIDE'S PEACH PIE
Kathleen Clark, Springfield, Ohio

Since my daughter, Beth, and her husband, Gary, do not care for cake, they opted for a "wedding pie" on their special day. Family and friends made 75 pies, many of which were set on a tiered holder to resemble a tall wedding cake. This is Beth's favorite.

Pastry for a double-crust pie (9 inches)
    5 cups sliced peeled peaches
    1 tablespoon lemon juice
    1/2 cup sugar
    1/4 cup packed brown sugar
    3 tablespoons all-purpose flour
    1/4 teaspoon ground nutmeg
    1/8 teaspoon salt
    1/2 teaspoon almond extract
    2 tablespoons butter *or* margarine, cubed

Line a 9-in. pie plate with bottom crust; trim pastry even with edge and set aside. In a bowl, toss peaches with lemon juice. Combine the sugars, flour, nutmeg and salt; add to peaches and toss. Sprinkle with almond extract; toss gently. Transfer to prepared crust; dot with butter. Roll out remaining pastry to fit top of pie; place over filling. Cut slits in pastry. Trim, seal and flute edges. Cover edge loosely with foil. Bake at 425° for 15 minutes. Reduce heat to 350°; remove foil and bake for 45-50 minutes longer or until crust is golden brown and filling is bubbly. Cool on a wire rack. **Yield:** 6-8 servings.

FRUIT PIE CRUMB TOPPING
Kathleen Clark, Springfield, Ohio

My mother always sprinkled on this wonderful crumb topping to dress up her two-crust fruit pies. The topping not only looks pretty, it provides a crisp contrast to the soft fruit filling. I used it to top pies for my daughter's wedding reception.

Tip: *Prepare and refrigerate up to 2 days before baking pies.*

    1/2 cup all-purpose flour
    1/4 cup sugar
    1/4 cup cold butter *or* margarine
Dash ground cinnamon, optional

In a small bowl, combine flour and sugar. Cut in butter until mixture resembles coarse crumbs. Sprinkle over fruit pies. Sprinkle with cinnamon if desired. **Yield:** 1 cup (topping for 2 pies).

FESTIVE SUGAR CUBES
Sheila Busch, Landis, Saskatchewan

The Western theme at our son Scott's wedding to Tammie was carried right down to the sugar cubes! I decorated the cute cubes with icing in the shape of horseshoes, cactus and cowboy hats and boots. Little details like this made their day even "sweeter".

    2 teaspoons meringue powder*
    2 tablespoons water
    1 cup confectioners' sugar
Food coloring of your choice
Pastry bag *or* heavy-duty resealable plastic bag

Assorted small pastry tips
  60 to 80 sugar cubes

In a small mixing bowl, combine meringue powder and water. Beat on high speed until well mixed. Add confectioners' sugar; beat until the mixture is fluffy and soft peaks form. Tint icing with food coloring or divide in half and tint each portion. Cut a small hole in the corner of pastry or plastic bag; insert pastry tip. Fill bag with icing; pipe each sugar cube with a design. Let sugar cubes dry at room temperature for 8 hours or overnight before storing in airtight containers. **Yield:** 60-80 servings. ***Editor's Note:** Meringue powder can be found in cake decorating supply stores or by mail order. (See Cake Decorating Resource, p. 48.)

CREAMY PASTEL MINTS
Jamie Gurney, Odessa, Missouri

David and I hosted a delicious dinner at my parents' house after our outdoor ceremony at a scenic spot. Our guests appreciated a tray of pretty, refreshing mints after the hearty meal. These mints are easy to make and have wonderful homemade flavor.

  1 package (8 ounces) cream cheese,
    softened
  1 teaspoon mint extract
6-2/3 cups confectioners' sugar
Red, green and yellow food coloring
Sugar

In a small mixing bowl, beat cream cheese and mint extract until smooth. Gradually beat in as much confectioners' sugar as possible; knead in remaining confectioners' sugar. Divide mixture into four portions. Tint one pink, one green and one yellow, leaving one portion white. For each color, shape into 1/2-in. balls. Dip one side of each ball into sugar. Press sugared side into small candy molds; unmold and place on waxed paper. Let stand 1 hour or until dry before storing in airtight containers; refrigerate. May be stored for up to 1 week before serving. **Yield:** about 12-1/2 dozen. **Editor's Note:** Mints may also be made without molds by placing sugar side up on waxed paper. Flatten with a fork, forming a crisscross pattern.

COCONUT CREAM PIE
Gertrude Gojmerac
Souris, Prince Edward Island

After their wedding in a small country church, our daughter Angela and her husband, Lonnie Robertson, were driven to the reception in a horse-drawn wagon—along the same route that Angela's great-grandparents took in the 1800s! Later, the guests raved over luscious desserts like this old-fashioned pie.

2/3 cup sugar
1/4 cup cornstarch
  2 tablespoons all-purpose flour
1/4 teaspoon salt
  3 cups milk
  3 egg yolks, beaten
  1 tablespoon butter *or* margarine
  2 teaspoons vanilla extract
  1 cup flaked coconut, *divided*
  2 cups whipped cream *or* whipped
    topping
  1 pastry shell (9 inches), baked

In a saucepan, combine sugar, cornstarch, flour and salt; gradually add milk until smooth. Bring to a boil over medium heat. Cook and stir for 2 minutes or until thickened. Remove from the heat. Gradually stir a small amount into egg yolks; return all to the pan, stirring constantly. Bring to a gentle boil; cook and stir for 2 minutes. Remove from the heat; stir in butter and vanilla. Cool to lukewarm; fold in 2/3 cup coconut. Pour into pastry shell. Refrigerate until set, about 3 hours. Meanwhile, toast the remaining coconut. To serve, top with whipped cream and sprinkle with toasted coconut. Store in the refrigerator. **Yield:** 6-8 servings.

CHOCOLATE COFFEE SPOONS
Toni Swanson, Gull Lake, Saskatchewan

My husband, Mark, and I gave our wedding guests these cute spoons as favors. They're a fun way to flavor an out-of-the-ordinary cup of coffee. Plus, the plastic spoon handles can be color-coordinated with any bridal theme.

  Tip: *For variety, use cherry or cinnamon candy flavoring, as well as the mint.*

  1 pound dark *or* milk chocolate candy
    coating*, broken into small pieces
1/4 teaspoon mint candy flavoring*
    (oil-based only), optional
  60 plastic spoons

Place 1/4 pound candy coating in a deep glass or plastic cup. Microwave at 30% or 50% power for 1 minute or until melted, stirring every 30 seconds. Stir in flavoring if desired. Coat entire bowl of a plastic spoon with chocolate. Place on a waxed paper-lined baking sheet. Repeat until all spoons are coated. Refrigerate until firm, about 10 minutes. Cover and store in a cool place until ready to serve. **Yield:** 60 servings. ***Editor's Note:** Dark or milk chocolate candy coating is found in the baking section of most grocery stores and is often sold in bulk packages of 1 to 1-1-2 pounds. This recipe was tested in a 700-watt microwave. Candy flavoring can be found in cake decorating supply stores or by mail order. (See Cake Decorating Resource, p. 48.)

Horseshoes Take Wedding Cake to New Heights!

What could be a more fitting finale for a wedding feast served with down-home hospitality than a memory-making dessert like this lovely and luscious cake?

Combining elegance and country charm, this crowd-pleasing confection was created by our food editors using recipes and ideas from some of the brides and grooms featured in this book.

Its simple yet special trims include three horseshoe-shaped layers, frosting in an eye-catching basket-weave pattern and colorful blooms tucked around and on top. Plus, it's *not* tricky to assemble.

Your guests will rave over this show-stopping sweet that tastes as good as it looks!

HORSESHOE-LAYER WEDDING CAKE
Donna Rhinesmith, Kirksville, Missouri

My husband, Richard, and I "got hitched" in a little country church. His sister, Donna Epperson, made our wedding cake using this delicious white cake recipe. It's moist with wonderful homemade taste and texture.

Baking pans—two 6-inch round, two 10-inch round, two 14-inch round and six 12-inch horseshoe-shaped (see Cake Decorating Resource on p. 48)
Waxed paper
   3 cups butter (no substitutes), softened, *divided*
   3 cups shortening, *divided*
   18 cups sugar, *divided*
   24 cups all-purpose flour, *divided*
   12 tablespoons baking powder, *divided*
   6 teaspoons salt, *divided*
   12 cups milk, *divided*
   6 cups egg whites (about 48 large eggs), *divided*
   4 tablespoons vanilla extract, *divided*
   1 cardboard cake base (6-inch round)
Bridal Cake Frosting (recipe above right)
   2 round separator plates (one 14 inches and one 12 inches)
   3 covered boards (two 16-inch square and one 20-inch square)
   2 pastry *or* heavy-duty resealable plastic bags
Pastry tips—#48 basket weave and #21 star
   4 Grecian spiked pillars (7 inches)
   4 Grecian spiked pillars (9 inches)
Dowel rod (3-feet x 1/4-inch diameter)
Silk *or* edible fresh flowers

Line baking pans with waxed paper; grease and flour waxed paper and set aside. **Note:** Cakes may need to be baked in batches depending on number of pans and oven space available.

In a large mixing bowl, cream 3/4 cup butter, 3/4 cup shortening and 4-1/2 cups sugar. Combine 6 cups flour, 3 tablespoons baking powder and 1-1/2 teaspoons salt; add to creamed mixture alternately with 3 cups milk. Beat on medium speed

for 2 minutes. In another mixing bowl, beat 1-1/2 cups egg whites and 1 tablespoon vanilla until stiff peaks form. Fold into batter. Repeat three times. Pour into prepared pans, filling each 6-in. pan with 2 cups batter, each 10-in. pan with 6 cups batter and each horseshoe-shaped pan with 4 cups batter. Bake the 6-in., 10-in. and horseshoe cakes at 350° for 30-35 minutes or until a toothpick inserted near the center comes out clean. Fill each 14-in. pan with 10 cups batter. Bake 14-in. cakes at 325° for 50-55 minutes or until cakes test done. Cool in pans for 10 minutes before removing to wire racks to cool completely. Level tops of cakes. **Yield:** 60 cups batter.

BRIDAL CAKE FROSTING
Joanne Leistico, Elk River, Minnesota

I've made wedding cakes for 15 years. I use box mixes but created my own frosting recipe. It has a nice flavor, plus it pipes and sets up well. I used this frosting on the cake when our daughter, Delores, married cowboy Les Jensen.

   10 cups shortening, *divided*
   35 cups confectioners' sugar (about 10 pounds), *divided*
   2-1/2 cups milk, *divided*
   10 teaspoons vanilla extract, *divided*
   5 teaspoons almond extract, *divided*

In a large mixing bowl, cream 2 cups shortening. Gradually beat in 7 cups confectioners' sugar. Add 1/2 cup milk; beat until light and fluffy. Beat in 2 teaspoons vanilla and 1 teaspoon almond extract. Repeat four times. Store in the refrigerator. Bring to room temperature before decorating cake. **Yield:** 40 cups.

To Begin Decorating the Cake:

Each frosted layer of the wedding cake consists of two cakes with frosting in between. Place one 6-in. cake on 6-in. cake base; spread with frosting to within 1/2 in. of edge. Place second cake on top. Frost top and sides with a thin layer of frosting to coat crumbs. With additional frosting, frost top smooth. Place 10-in. cake on the 12-in. separator plate and one 14-in. cake on the 20-in. covered board. Frost and layer following the directions for the 6-in. cake.

Place one horseshoe cake on the 14-in. separator plate and each of the 16-in. covered boards. Frost and layer following the directions for the 6-in. cake. Also frost the sides of the horseshoe cakes, smoothing with an icing knife until surfaces are flat.

For Basket-Weave Design: (see diagram on the next page)

Cut a small hole in the corner of pastry or plas- ↪

tic bag; insert basket weave tip. Fill bag with frosting. Pipe one vertical line down the side of the 14-in. cake. Working from the top edge, cover the vertical line with 1-1/2-in. horizontal lines, leaving 1/2 in. space between each. Pipe another vertical line to the right of the first vertical line, overlapping ends of horizontal lines. Starting to the right of the first vertical line, pipe 1-1/2-in. horizontal lines over second vertical line to fill open spaces. Repeat process until entire side of cake is covered with basket-weave design. Repeat procedure for 10-in. and 6-in. layer cakes.

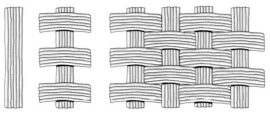

For Rope Border: (see diagram below)

Prepare another bag; insert star tip. Fill bag with frosting. Touch tip to top edge of the 14-in. layer cake. Pipe frosting down, up and around to the right forming an "S" curve. Tuck tip under bottom arch of first "S" and repeat procedure. Continue joining "S" curves to form a rope border. Repeat on bottom edge. Pipe a rope border on top and bottom edges of each horseshoe cake.

To Assemble Cake:

Mark pillar placement by centering the separator plate with the horseshoe cake over the 14-in. layer cake; gently press onto cake surface. Lift plate off. Repeat procedure with 12-in. separator plate over the horseshoe cake. Insert 7-in. pillars into marks on 14-in. cake and 9-in. pillars into marks on the horseshoe cake.

Cut dowel into six pieces, about 1/8 in. above the height of 10-in. cake. Insert dowels 1 to 2 in. apart into 10-in. cake center to support 6-in. layer cake. Center and place the 6-in. cake on top of the 10-in. layer cake. To assemble, place separator plate with the horseshoe cake on the 7-in. pillars. Center separator plate with 6-in. and 10-in. tiered cake on the 9-in. pillars. Pipe rope border along top and bottom edges of 6-in. and 10-in. layer cakes. Arrange one horseshoe cake on each side of wedding cake. Decorate cakes with flowers. **Yield:** about 200 servings. **Editor's Note:** Decorated cake does not need refrigeration.

HORSESHOE LAYERS highlighted the wedding cake of Brook and Keith Hickle of Enumclaw, Washington. Five round cakes formed the base for three graduated tiers of horseshoe-shaped cakes. This design inspired the cake our food editors created.

EGG-CELLENT IDEAS

Leftover egg yolks may be used in custards, egg dishes and to enrich sauces. To refrigerate, cover whole yolks with water in an airtight container and refrigerate for up to 2 days. To freeze, combine 1/4 cup egg yolks (4 yolks) with 1/2 teaspoon sugar or 1/8 teaspoon salt. (Use sugar for sweet dishes and salt for savory dishes.) Cover, label and freeze for up to 1 year. To use frozen egg yolks in sauces, custards and other egg dishes, thaw in refrigerator and substitute 1 tablespoon for 1 large yolk and 3 tablespoons for 1 large egg.

Cake Decorating Resource

Various sizes of cake pans, including the horseshoe-shaped pan used in our White Wedding Cake recipe, plus flavorings, paste food coloring and meringue powder can be obtained by mail from Wilton Industries, Inc., 2240 W. 75th St., Woodridge IL 60517. Their customer orders telephone number is 1-800/794-5866. Fax: 1-888/824-9520.

Check out their helpful Web site at *Wilton.com*. On-line information is available at *Catalog@wilton.com* or *Info@wilton.com*.

Canadians can contact Wilton Industries, Canada, Ltd., 98 Carrier Dr., Etobicoke ON Canada M9W 5R1. Phone: 1-416/679-0790. Fax 1-416/679-0798.

On-line information is available in Canada at *canadasales@wilton.ca*

Classic Country Cakes

Celebrating the sweet sentiments of a wedding is, well…a piece of cake. Plain or fancy, these memorable confections can't be topped when it comes to heart-felt ingredients. Have a taste!

FIT TO BE TIED in Winfield, West Virginia, Jessica and Shawn Hoffman's wedding cake was wrapped in true cowboy fashion with striking red bandannas, icing ropes, corralled ponies and a two-stepping couple on the top.

SPOKE-N FOR. Setting the wheels of their reception in motion are Crystal and Brandon Shane Martin. "The groom's German chocolate cake was shaped like a wagon wheel," says his mom, Margaret, from Helotes, Texas. The motif continued with chuck wagon buffet tables.

TIERS OF JOY attest that love's in bloom for Tammy and Steve Didier from Elk City, Idaho. Their garden-variety cake was garnished with brightly colored hand-picked carnations, roses and foliage. The cowpoke on the top layer, with his mini lariat and Stetson hat, stands for the groom's ranching background.

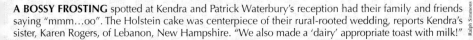

BALES OF FUN were forked over in a dessert designed for Jill and Ed Shramek. "From a photo of Ed's hay truck, the crafty baker created a cream-filled chocolate cake, then piped on colored frosting using a basket-weave tip. Peppermint patties formed the tires," the bride writes from their Powell, Wyoming home.

A BOSSY FROSTING spotted at Kendra and Patrick Waterbury's reception had their family and friends saying "mmm…oo". The Holstein cake was centerpiece of their rural-rooted wedding, reports Kendra's sister, Karen Rogers, of Lebanon, New Hampshire. "We also made a 'dairy' appropriate toast with milk!"

Cake Puts Groom's Best Foot Forward

Something sweet was afoot when Traci Renner and Chad Betts of Baltic, Ohio (far right) exchanged rural "I do's" at his parents' country acreage.

Chad's mom tastefully captured the couple's Western theme with the confections she created—two cowboy boot-shaped groom's cakes that were "roped" to the main tiered cake.

Our food editors liked the clever motif so much they decided to duplicate the boot (below). The recipe for this rich chocolaty cake comes from Darlene Nelson of Portal, North Dakota.

Using the full-size pattern and sim-

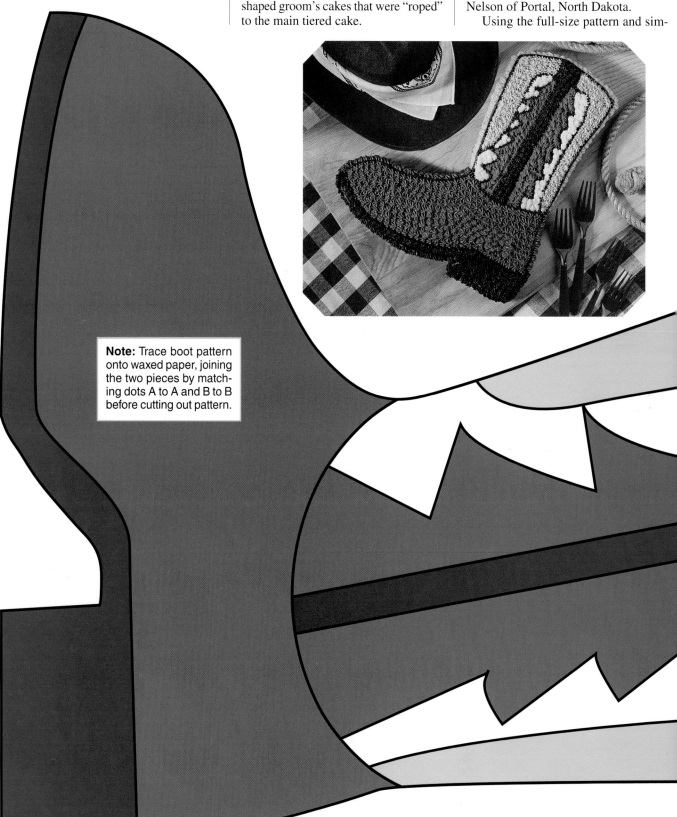

Note: Trace boot pattern onto waxed paper, joining the two pieces by matching dots A to A and B to B before cutting out pattern.

ple-to-follow decorating instructions here, you can easily tailor a boot cake to match your wedding colors. It's sure to be a "shoe-in" for compliments on your big day!

GROOM'S BOOT CAKE

1/2 cup butter (no substitutes), softened
1-1/2 cups sugar
3 eggs
1-1/2 teaspoons vanilla extract
2-1/4 cups all-purpose flour
6 tablespoons baking cocoa
1-1/2 teaspoons baking powder
1-1/2 teaspoons baking soda
1/2 teaspoon salt
1-1/2 cups buttermilk
3 cups Cream Cheese Frosting (page 53) or Bridal Cake

Note: See Cake Decorating Resource, p. 48, to find cake decorating supplies.

Frosting (page 47)
1 tablespoon milk
Brown and blue paste food coloring
5 pastry or small heavy-duty resealable plastic bags
Pastry tips #5 round and #21 star

In a mixing bowl, cream butter and sugar. Add eggs, one at a time, beating well after each addition. Beat on high speed until light and fluffy. Beat in vanilla. Combine the flour, cocoa, baking powder, baking soda and salt; add to creamed mixture alternately with buttermilk. Beat on low just until combined. Line a 13-in. x 9-in. x 2-in. baking pan with waxed paper; grease and flour paper. Pour batter into prepared pan. Bake at 350° for 25 minutes or until a toothpick inserted near the center comes out clean. Cool

IN STEP with their Western theme, Traci and Chad Betts showcased frosted cowboy boots "tied" to a tiered wedding cake trimmed with love knots.

for 10 minutes; remove from pan to wire rack to cool completely.

Level the top of cake. Trace boot pattern onto waxed paper as directed on pattern and cut out. Place pattern on cake and cut around pattern. Place boot cake on a large serving platter or 16-in.-square covered board. Prepare frosting. Combine 1/2 cup frosting with milk to make a glaze; evenly spread over top and sides of boot. Refrigerate for 20-25 minutes or until completely set.

Cut apart waxed paper boot pattern along inside design lines and reposition pattern on cake. Using a toothpick, lightly trace around each piece to transfer patterns.

Tint 3/4 cup frosting brown. Tint 1 cup dark blue and 1/2 cup light blue. Leave 1/4 cup white. Cover and refrigerate blue and white frostings. Cut a small hole in the corner of a pastry or plastic bag; insert round tip. Fill bag with brown frosting. Following the pattern, outline boot shape and inside design lines with brown frosting. Insert star tip in brown frosting bag. Pipe stars on top and sides of brown pattern areas as shown in photo at far left.

Prepare another pastry or plastic bag, inserting star tip. Fill bag with white frosting; pipe stars on white areas. Insert star tip into another pastry or plastic bag; fill with light blue frosting. Pipe stars on top and sides of light blue areas of cake. Insert star tip into pastry or plastic bag; fill with dark blue frosting. Pipe stars on top and sides of dark blue area of cake. Store cake in the refrigerator. **Yield:** 12-16 servings. **Editor's Note:** Use of coupler rings will allow you to easily change tip from bag to bag.

Wedding Cakes Come in Many Flavors

ANGEL FOOD CAKE
Marilyn Niemeyer, Doon, Iowa

For our daughter Briana's marriage to Jed Van Der Zwaag, a friend made this lovely, airy cake from a recipe she's used for over 45 years.

1 cup cake flour
1-1/2 cups sugar, *divided*
1-1/4 cups egg whites (about 10 eggs)
1-1/4 teaspoons cream of tartar
1 teaspoon vanilla extract
1/4 teaspoon almond extract
1/4 teaspoon salt

Combine cake flour and 1/2 cup sugar; set aside. In a mixing bowl, beat egg whites, cream of tartar, extracts and salt on high speed until foamy. Gradually add remaining sugar, 2 tablespoons at a time, beating until stiff peaks form. Gently fold in reserved flour mixture, about 1/3 cup at a time. Gently pour into an ungreased 10-in. tube pan. Carefully run a knife through batter to remove air pockets. Bake at 350° for 35-40 minutes or until cake springs back when lightly touched and cracks feel dry. Immediately invert pan; cool completely. Run a knife around edge and center tube to loosen; remove cake to a wire rack to cool completely. **Yield:** 12-16 servings.

CARROT CAKE
Shannon Walker, Thermopolis, Wyoming

Mark and I planned to be wed on a mountain on a friend's ranch, but a snowstorm sent us to our alternate plan—a local country museum. Our friend Sandy Howe made a sheet cake using this recipe. Chockfull of nuts, pineapple and coconut, it's our favorite.

2 cups sugar
1-1/2 cups vegetable oil
1 teaspoon vanilla extract
2 cups all-purpose flour
2 teaspoons ground cinnamon
1 teaspoon baking soda
1/2 teaspoon salt
3 eggs, beaten
2 cups finely shredded carrots
1 cup flaked coconut
1 can (8 ounces) crushed pineapple, drained
1 cup chopped pecans, *divided*
Cream Cheese Frosting (recipe above right)

In a mixing bowl, beat sugar, oil and vanilla. Combine the flour, cinnamon, baking soda and salt; add to the sugar mixture alternately with eggs. Mix well. Stir in carrots, coconut, pineapple and 1/2 cup pecans. Pour into a greased and floured 13-in. x 9-in. x 2-in. baking pan. Bake at 350° for 40-45 minutes or until a toothpick inserted near the center comes out clean. Cool for 10 minutes; remove from pan to a wire rack to cool completely. Frost with Cream Cheese Frosting. Garnish with remaining nuts. Store in the refrigerator. **Yield:** 12-16 servings.

CREAM CHEESE FROSTING
Sharon Lugdon, Costigan, Maine

This smooth, versatile frosting has a delicate vanilla flavor. The woman who made the wedding cake for our daughter, Leanne, and her groom, Billy Waters, used this recipe. It's also excellent on carrot cake.

2 packages (3 ounces *each*) cream cheese, softened
1/2 cup butter (no substitutes), softened
2 teaspoons vanilla extract
1/4 teaspoon salt
5 to 6 cups confectioners' sugar

In a mixing bowl, beat cream cheese, butter, vanilla and salt until smooth. Gradually beat in confectioners' sugar. Store frosting in the refrigerator. **Yield:** about 3 cups.

STRAWBERRY CAKE
Pam Anderson, Billings, Montana

This fresh-tasting cake with its pretty pink tint took center stage at the reception for my farmer cousin, Scott Kittelmann, and his wife, Kathy.

1 package (18-1/4 ounces) white cake mix
1 package (3 ounces) strawberry gelatin
1 cup water
1/2 cup vegetable oil
4 egg whites
1/2 cup mashed unsweetened strawberries
Whipped cream *or* frosting of your choice

In a mixing bowl, combine the first four ingredients. Beat on low speed for 1 minute or until moistened; beat on medium for 4 minutes. In another mixing bowl, beat egg whites until stiff peaks form. Fold egg whites and mashed strawberries into cake batter. Pour into three greased and floured 8-in. round baking pans. Bake at 350° for 25-30 minutes or until a toothpick comes out clean. Cool for 10 minutes; remove from pans to wire racks to cool completely. Frost with whipped cream or frosting. **Yield:** 12-16 servings.

FLUFFY WHITE FROSTING
Martha Mills, Walterboro, South Carolina

When our son, Chris, and his wife, Kim, tied the knot on our land in the country, I made their cake and frosted it with this light buttery frosting.

    1/4 cup cornstarch
    2 cups cold water
    2 cups butter (no substitutes), softened
    2 cups sugar
    2 teaspoons almond extract

In a saucepan, combine cornstarch and water until smooth. Bring to a boil over medium heat. Cook and stir for 2 minutes or until thickened. Refrigerate for 1 hour. In a mixing bowl, cream butter and sugar. Beat in almond extract. Add cornstarch mixture and beat until sugar is dissolved and frosting is fluffy. Frost cake immediately; store in the refrigerator. **Yield:** about 6-1/2 cups.

BANANA CAKE
Patsy Hood, Nemo, South Dakota

When our daughter, Robbyn, married Ronald Slavin, two boot-shaped cakes flanked their traditional cake. Ronald requested that one be his favorite—banana.

    1 package (18-1/4 ounces) yellow cake
      mix
    1 package (3.4 ounces) instant banana
      pudding mix
    1-1/4 cups water
    1/3 cup vegetable oil
    2 eggs
    2 teaspoons banana flavoring*
Frosting of your choice

In a mixing bowl, combine the dry cake and pudding mixes, water, oil, eggs and flavoring. Beat on low speed for 1 minute or until moistened; beat on medium for 4 minutes. Line a 13-in. x 9-in. x 2-in. baking pan with waxed paper; grease and flour paper. Pour batter into prepared pan. Bake at 350° for 30-35 minutes or until a toothpick inserted near the center comes out clean. Cool in pan 10 minutes; remove from pan to a wire rack to cool completely. Frost. **Yield:** 12-16 servings. ***Editor's Note:** Banana flavoring is available at cake decorating and candy supply stores.

RICH CHOCOLATE FROSTING
Amy Via, North Richland Hills, Texas

My husband, Doug, loved his chocolate groom's cake (left) that was topped with this smooth, creamy frosting and accented with chocolate-covered strawberries. Some were made to look like tuxedos (see directions below).

    2 cups butter (no substitutes), softened
    9 cups confectioners' sugar
    2-1/2 cups baking cocoa
    1 teaspoon vanilla extract
    1 to 1-1/2 cups milk

In a large mixing bowl, cream butter. Gradually beat in confectioners' sugar, cocoa and vanilla. Add enough milk until frosting reaches spreading consistency. **Yield:** about 8 cups.

TUXEDO STRAWBERRIES

    18 medium fresh strawberries
    1 cup vanilla or white chips
    3-1/2 teaspoons shortening, *divided*
    1-1/3 cups semisweet chocolate chips
Pastry bag or small heavy-duty resealable
      plastic bag
#2 pastry tip, optional

Line a tray or baking sheet with waxed paper; set aside. Wash berries and pat completely dry. In microwave, melt vanilla chips and 1-1/2 teaspoons shortening. Dip each berry until two-thirds is coated (see Fig. 1), allowing excess to drip off. Place on tray; chill 30 minutes or until set. Melt chocolate chips and remaining shortening. Dip each side of berry into chocolate from the tip of the strawberry to the top of vanilla coating (see Figs. 2 and 3). Set aside remaining chocolate. Chill berries for 30 minutes or until set. Melt reserved chocolate if necessary. Cut a small hole in the corner of a pastry or plastic bag; insert tip or pipe directly from bag. Fill with melted chocolate. Pipe a "bow tie" at the top of the white "v" and two or three buttons down the front of the "shirt" (see Fig. 4). Chill for 30 minutes or until set. Cover and store in the refrigerator for 1 day. **Yield:** 1-1/2 dozen.

Fig. 1 Forming shirt

Fig. 2 Forming first half of jacket

Fig. 3 Forming second half of jacket

Fig. 4 Forming bow tie and buttons

Ranch Gal, Farm Boy Make Country Connection

To welcome her new cowboy, Brian McKay, into the family, Kathy Konz's folks hosted a swingin' shindig at their Republic, Washington ranch.

RIDING HIGH after tying the knot, Kathy and Brian McKay trotted off into the sunset on her family's guest ranch in Republic, Washington. "We met at a local rodeo and spent our courtship days team roping," Kathy affirms. "Over 500 guests wished us 'happy trails'."

A SMOOTH-AS-SILK wedding day gave Kathy and her attendants reason to beam on the barn staircase. She shares, "The cowboy groomsmen escorted the gals up the path to the front deck of my parents' log home for the ceremony."

Photos: Nick Foliger, Spokane, Wash.

LOVE'S ALOFT at the rollicking reception where a warmly-lit hayloft was packed to the rafters with dancers, a live band and plenty of Old-West decor.

"HOWDY, PARDNERS!" Cowboys on horseback directed traffic, greeted guests and escorted a Percheron-pulled surrey carrying Kathy and her dad.

ALL'S FARE. Family and friends "parked" the fixin's for a barbecue in an airy carport. After digging into the buffet and a watering trough full of beverages, guests headed outside to picnic tables.

FOOTLOOSE FUN was had by all dancing their boots off on a brand-new barn floor finished just 3 days before Kathy and Brian took the big step.

A TENDER ENTRANCE was made by Kathy and her father from a fairy tale-like carriage. Practice makes perfect for the bridal delivery (see inset)! Their guests looked on from 60 log benches hewed by the bride's brother.

4-H Ideals Shine at Western Wedding

HEAD, heart, hands and health—the four H's in 4-H Club—took on special meaning the day Krista Rawie and Rob Castell were wed at her folks' Abiqua Creek Ranch in Silverton, Oregon.

"Krista has been active in 4-H since she was a young girl," notes mother-of-the-bride Sandi Rawie. "At 18, she became a 4-H leader, teaching those same rural values to other kids.

"So when she got engaged, it was no surprise that she wanted a country wedding—with a little help from her 4-H 'family'."

The couple chose a picturesque place for their ceremony—a grove of lush fir trees with the Abiqua River flowing by and majestic Mt. Hood in the distance.

"We added to that natural beauty by filling cattle troughs with cascading blooms and scattering straw bales around," Sandi reports. "And we topped fence posts along our driveway with Western hats banded with burgundy ribbon and bandannas."

As guests arrived, they stopped to sign the guest book on a wooden stand handmade by the groom. Then they were seated on borrowed benches trimmed with burgundy raffia bows.

Among them were Krista's 4-H kids, all dressed in matching western vests. "It was their job to signal Rob, who rode up over the pasture knoll on his horse as we all watched," Sandi shares.

Krista and her father made their grand entrance in a horse-drawn carriage. Wearing a Victorian-style prairie dress and Western hat with veil, the beaming bride joined her tuxedoed groom under a cedar arch "Hitchin' Post" crafted by Rob.

Obviously, it took many heads and hands to pull off this event that united two hearts for a lifetime of health and happiness!

Their Hall Was All Decked Out...

♥ We draped the walls of the reception hall with rolls of burgundy plastic table runners, tying up 20-foot sections with burgundy and white bandannas for a scalloped effect.

♥ An old two-seater wagon held the wedding gifts. A mail pouch made from burlap was hung on it to collect the cards.

♥ Our farrier gave us old horseshoes to use in our table decor. After Rob welded pairs of horseshoes together, we sat them atop miniature bales of straw (found in craft stores). Then we poked dried flowers into each bale.

♥ For centerpieces, I gathered old cowboy boots from rummage sales. We spray-painted them in wedding colors and tied lace around the neck of each boot. We tucked floral foam into the top of the boots, then arranged bouquets of dried flowers, wheat and oats.

—Sandi Rawie

HAPPY TRAILS to Krista and Rob Castell's ranch wedding were blazed by hats on fences (left). The groom made a boot-shaped guest book stand (far left) and a cedar hitchin' post (above). Fringe accented the burgundy and forest green bridesmaids' Western dresses (top).

SOMETHINGS OLD AND NEW gave this union a timeless air. The carriage (center) rolled the bride and her dad to her promising future. Antique wheels (left) held gifts, and tiny toy horses pulled a flower wagon on the table (above).

Couple Puts Southwest Spin on Special Day

A WESTERN WEDDING with a little zest was just what Kim Earl ordered for her big day!

"Kim has shown quarter horses since she was 9 years old. She used to joke that she would have a Western wedding even if it meant getting married at a horse show by the judge during lunch break," mother-of-the-bride Sandy Earl reminisces with a laugh.

Fittingly, Kim and Mike Fraley tied the knot at the Earls' home in Tiffin, Ohio in front of the riding arena—while the horses looked on! Even the family rottweiler and terrier got into the spirit of the occasion by sporting bandannas as they greeted guests.

Dressed in true Western fashion, Mike and his groomsmen wore Wranglers, cowboy hats and boots. Kim walked down the grassy aisle on her father's arm wearing an antique lace dress and carrying a silk bouquet with rope accents.

Her bridesmaids modeled terra cotta-colored velveteen gowns that were trimmed with metal studs around the collars and cuffs.

By choosing desert colors, cactus and coyote table toppers and a south-of-the-border menu, the creative couple added a definite Southwestern flair to their ceremony.

The weathered timber arch where Kim and Mike exchanged vows sported a bleached steer skull, plus barrels with flower arrangements in vibrant shades of desert sunset.

After the ceremony, guests moved to the 40- x 120-foot tent that shaded heavily ladened buffet tables draped with brightly woven blankets.

"We served salsa and chips as appetizers," reports Sandy, "along with a hog roast, two sides of shredded beef, Spanish rice, cheese enchiladas, potato salad and baked beans."

The twosome's tiered wedding cake was frosted in a basket weave pattern similar to the look on Kim's saddle. Smaller cakes were shaped like boots and hay bales and accented with tiny cowboy hats, clay pots and other Southwestern details.

"It was a beautiful day," Sandy recalls. "All of our family and friends had a wonderful time enjoying our Southwestern fling—without having to worry about beating that Southwest heat!"

SOUTH-OF-THE-BORDER touches, such as cactus and coyote table toppers and cowboy boot lights strung along the table, added plenty of zip to Kim and Mike Fraley's outdoor wedding. Some tasty accents guests enjoyed were the barrels of peanuts near the head table.

COUNTRY-STYLE was in fashion at Kim and Mike's celebration! The bridal party put on Western wear, right down to the young ring bearer, and guests followed suit. The buffet tables were draped in serapes and served up spicy eats.

BRIDLE SITE. Choosing the perfect spot to tie the knot was a cinch for Kim, an avid rider. She and Mike exchanged vows on her parents' spread, under an arch trimmed in equine accents, while friends, family and horses watched.

POND-SIDE BRIDE, former Dairy Princess Penny Snyder, shares a romantic moment with groom Dave (left) and in a barn swing (above). Her mother made the cute cow cake topper (below).

Romantic Day for This Farmer's Daughter Was Dairy Delightful!

THE SPECIAL CEREMONY Penny and Dave Snyder planned for their nuptials near Brogue, Pennsylvania was "udderly" country!

"We were milking by 4 a.m. so we'd have time to prepare for the wedding," says dairy farm wife and mother-of-the-bride Lois Jordan.

"By 6 o'clock, friends arrived to set up straw bales as benches under the oak trees in our heifer pasture...and flanked the 'aisle' with milk cans to serve as flower stands.

"We were thrilled to see how pretty the attendants' rich magenta dresses (made by a family friend) looked when the bridal party assembled in our leafy 'cathedral' setting.

"But it was a calf called 'Clover', led by a junior bridesmaid, who really stole the show!" Lois laughs "She was listed in the wedding program as simply a 'friend of the bride'."

Bales of fun were had by all 21 in the wedding party as Penny's dad, Bob, treated them to a "limousine" ride in a colorfully decorated tractor-drawn hay wagon back to the barn reception...

where homemade hospitality flowed by the gallons.

"Along with plenty of barbecued pork and covered dishes brought by guests, we served beverages from milk cans," details Lois.

The charming farm atmosphere focused on a bevy of bossies "rounded up" on walls and crossbeams. Other accents included bright bouquets of helium balloons tied to milk bottles and filled with salt to anchor them to the informal dining tables.

Following the meal, the bride swung into action by tossing her bridal bouquet from the barn swing. And the children were invited to take a swing at a cow pinata crafted by the bride.

"As a special touch, I fashioned two collages from snapshots of Penny and Dave and mounted them on the silo," Lois notes. "Guests wrote personal messages around the borders. They now have a place of honor hanging in the newlyweds' living room."

No doubt this couple will cherish the memento of their rural romance until the cows come home...and long after!

Decor and More...

♥ A mailbox with the couple's names painted on the side made a perfect container for wedding cards.

♥ Old canning jars filled with flowers and topped with small votive cups served as fun homespun candle holders.

♥ A unique way to display the bridesmaids' bouquets was on wall hooks behind the head table.

♥ Old barn beams looked beautiful wrapped with garlands of tissue paper flowers that were intertwined with tiny white lights.—*Lois Jordan*

BOVINE BRIDESMAID! "Clover", a Holstein calf and friend of the bride, was led down the aisle by a junior attendant (top). Afterwards, the bridal party went for a ride in a hay wagon festooned with balloons (above)…while hungry guests dug into a hearty barnyard barbecue (below) and signed well wishes on the silo.

"PROMISE" LAND. Green pasture was grounds for beginning a life together for Penny and Dave (top). Hay benches, flowery milk cans (center) and wall-to-wall bossies added farm charm to a grade-A occasion.

Happiness Reins Her in...at Last!

" 'NO LASSO around my neck, no ring around my finger' is what I always said," chuckles Cindy Horsley Mason of Ellensburg, Washington. "That is, until I met *this* cowboy!

"I was 46 when Jerry and I were introduced at a horseback riding fund-raiser," recalls the fruit rancher's daughter. "A few months later, we were married.

"I was *terrified* of walking down the aisle," confides Cindy. "Jerry, a retired veterinarian who runs a cow/calf operation, agreed that a big church wedding wasn't for us.

"So when he suggested a wedding on horseback, I was thrilled. That way I could let 'Chino', my horse of 21 years, do the walking for me."

The ceremony was held in front of the Masons' log cabin verandah, which was lavishly decorated with cedar bough swags and wildflowers such as cattails and daisies tucked into milk cans. "I told Jerry's florist friends 'no roses'!" Cindy winks.

"We didn't send out invitations, just relied on people to spread the word that anyone who wanted to attend should come casually dressed.

"My friends were so glad to see me finally 'getting hitched' that they were eager to help out in any way that they could," she grins.

"Some 225 guests showed up! We seated them on hay bales in front of the cabin. A local rodeo posse (Jerry's a member) gave us a cowboy hat salute after we said our 'I do's'."

After the ceremony, Cindy changed from her Western-style white shirt and pants to a white skirt for dancing.

"For the reception, we topped picnic tables with cheery checked cloths, bushels of apples and old cowboy boots wrapped in bandannas, filled with wildflowers," she details.

"Our wedding cakes were decorated with frosted horseshoes and Jerry's Big M brand. We supplied the grilled steaks for dinner, but our friends provided the side dishes, main dishes and desserts...and even did some authentic

outdoor Dutch-oven cooking.

"While they took over, Jerry and I had a chance to sit back, relax and enjoy the 'ride'," smiles this bride whose dream-come-true wedding was definitely worth the wait!

A HIGH TIME was had by all when Cindy and Jerry Mason (left) found true love at last. A rodeo posse (above) gave a "hat's off" salute as the bride and groom entered on horseback. Their cake (top) was "branded" with frosting and sported a wire cowboy boot.

A FRONTIER FLAVOR spiced the Masons' log cabin wedding site that was brightened by flowers, boughs and bales. Dutch-oven dishes prepared by friends stacked up deliciously (above). Picnic tables were topped with the groom's flower-bedecked boots and sweet apples from the bride's family trees.

Make Your Wedding Dress—for under $100!

Do you want to keep your budget in line, yet still have a beautiful dress that will keep up with you on your big day? Here's the solution!

Our craft editor, Jane Craig, has designed and created a gorgeous gown that's simple to sew (no hemming is required), made of an eye-catching shimmery fabric and, best of all, can be assembled for *under $100*.

Lovely in its simplicity, this dress can be trimmed to suit your taste and to make it truly one of a kind. Plus, the dress is flattering yet practical for floating down a church aisle...or across a field or farmyard.

Jane also includes directions for a flouncy slip, optional detachable train and pretty headpiece.

With this dress, the trickiest part is trying to decide what to do with all the money you've saved!

Materials Needed (for two-piece dress with detachable train):

3-1/2 yards of 44-inch-wide pattern tracing paper with 1-inch grid or dots spaced 1 inch apart
18 yards of 41-inch-wide or wider blouse-weight fabric* (we used white 100% polyester crinkle)
Matching 7-inch skirt zipper
Matching all-purpose thread
10 inches of 5/8-inch-wide matching Velcro
6 hooks and eyes
1/2 yard of lightweight iron-on interfacing
Two 27.3 yard skeins of size 5 matching pearl cotton
Size 18 chenille needle
Quilter's marking pen or pencil
Standard sewing supplies

Materials Needed (for optional trims):

Fringe, lace or 3mm string pearl trim—5 yards plus distance around neckline and sleeves
5/8-inch-wide sheer satin-edge ribbon—5 yards plus distance around neckline and sleeves, plus 3/4 yard for each bow

* Yardage is approximate. For more accurate yardage, draw bodice and skirt/train patterns as directed. For each, multiply the length of the pattern x the number to cut. Calculate yardage and add 2 yards for bow for total yardage.

Description: Two-piece wedding dress has loose fitting self-lined bodice with boat neck and kimono sleeves. Self-lined skirt gathered to waistband has side seams and back zipper. Skirt and detachable train have horizontal tuck. Bow attaches to back of cummerbund. Neck and sleeve edges and tucks are trimmed with pearl cotton chain stitching.

Directions:

CUTTING: Bodice: Using measurements and adding ease as directed, draw bodice pattern onto pattern paper as illustrated in Fig. 1.

Cut four as directed on pattern for outside back, outside front, lining back and lining front.

Skirt: Draw skirt pattern onto pattern paper as shown in Fig. 2. Cut three as directed on pattern. Mark both stitching lines and fold of tuck onto right side of each skirt panel.

Train: Place pattern on doubled fabric with bottom of skirt pattern on crosswise fold and cut as directed. (Train will be twice the length of skirt pattern.)

Bow: Cut a 22-in.-wide x 72-in.-long piece of fabric.

CONSTRUCTION: Sew seams with right sides together and 1/2-in. seams unless otherwise directed.

Bodice: Sew outside bodice front and back together at shoulder seams, stitching from C to D. Then stitch front and back underarm/side seams. Clip curves and press seams open. Sew lining front and back together in same way.

Press 1/2 in. to wrong side on neck, sleeve and bottom edges of each.

Pin outside and lining together with wrong sides facing and folded edges and seams matching. Machine-stitch outside to lining, stitching around neckline through all layers as close as possible to folds. Then stitch around each sleeve opening and around bottom in same way.

Skirt: Sew long edges of two skirt panels together for center back seam, leaving an opening for the zipper at both ends of seam. Insert zipper into top of center back seam following the manufacturer's instructions.

Sew remaining skirt panel to back, matching long edges and markings for tuck. Press side seams open.

Fold fabric tube crosswise on marked fold of tuck with wrong sides together and seams and stitching lines of tuck aligned. Hand-baste through both layers

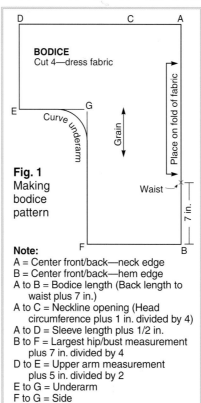

Fig. 1 Making bodice pattern

Note:
A = Center front/back—neck edge
B = Center front/back—hem edge
A to B = Bodice length (Back length to waist plus 7 in.)
A to C = Neckline opening (Head circumference plus 1 in. divided by 4)
A to D = Sleeve length plus 1/2 in.
B to F = Largest hip/bust measurement plus 7 in. divided by 4
D to E = Upper arm measurement plus 5 in. divided by 2
E to G = Underarm
F to G = Side

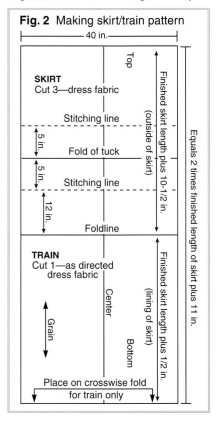

Fig. 2 Making skirt/train pattern

5-1/2 in. from fold, keeping fabric smooth and seams aligned.

Straight-stitch through both layers on matched stitching lines of tuck. Remove basting and open layers. Press fold of tuck toward bottom of skirt.

Pin raw edges of top and bottom of skirt together with wrong sides facing and seams and center markings matching. Length of skirt will be 1/2 in. longer than desired length.

Cut a 4-in.-wide piece of dress fabric x waist measurement plus 2 in. for the waistband. Also cut a 3-in.-wide piece of interfacing the same length as the waistband.

Center and fuse interfacing to wrong side of waistband following manufacturer's directions.

Fold waistband in half crosswise and mark fold for center front. Fold each end in to center and mark new folds for sides of waistband. Open waistband.

Fold waistband in half lengthwise with wrong sides together. Press fold. Open and press 1/2 in. to wrong side along one long edge.

Gather raw edges of skirt as one to fit long edge of waistband. Sew skirt to long raw edge of waistband, matching markings on band to center front and side seams of skirt. Zipper edge of back seam should be 1/2 in. from each end of waistband.

Fold waistband with right sides together along lengthwise fold, matching raw edges of each end. Stitch across each end. Trim seam and turn waistband right side out. Hand-sew folded edge of waistband to inside, covering seam.

Cut two 3-1/2-in.-long pieces of hook side of Velcro. Sew one centered along each end on outside of waistband. Band of train attaches here.

Hand-sew three hooks and eyes to inside ends of waistband so ends meet.

Train: On right side of train, mark fold of tuck 75-1/2 in. from one end of train. Then mark stitching lines 5 in. from each side of foldline. Stitch and press fold of tuck as for skirt.

Fold skirt pattern in half lengthwise on center line. Trim pattern, rounding corners of bottom end of pattern only. Open pattern.

Fold train crosswise with right sides of fabric together and edges matching. Pin rounded end of pattern to fold of train with grainlines matching. Mark outline of rounded end onto fabric.

Stitch around end of train on marking. Then stitch long edges of train together with a 1/4-in. seam. Trim rounded end 1/4 in. outside stitching. Clip curve. Turn right side out. Pin raw edges at top together with seams at sides. Press. ↷

GORGEOUS GOWN designed by Craft Editor Jane Craig is modeled by her daughter-in-law, Kathryn.

Gather and draw up top of train to 7-1/2 in. Cut a 4-in.-wide x 8-1/2-in.-long piece of dress fabric for band of train. Sew gathered edge of train to long edge of band. Finish band of train as for waistband of skirt.

Center and machine-sew a 7-in.-long piece of loop side of Velcro to underside of band.

Bow: Fold fabric for bow in half lengthwise to make a piece 11 in. wide for streamers. Stitch long edges together with a 1/4-in. seam, leaving opening for turning. Fold and press each end at a 45° angle. Open and stitch on pressed crease at each end. Trim fabric 1/4 in. outside stitching. Trim corners and points. Turn right side out. Hand-sew opening closed. Press.

From scraps, cut a 15-in. x 18-in. piece of fabric. Fold short edges of fabric wrong sides together with raw edges meeting in center to make piece 9 in. x 15 in. Fold remaining opposite raw edges in to center to make a 7-1/2-in. x 9-in. piece. Then fold short ends in to center to make a 7-1/2-in. x 4-1/2-in. piece. Hand-sew all layers together at center only.

Cut a 3-in. square of dress fabric for band of bow. Fold wrong sides together with edges meeting in center. Fold strip in half to make a 3/4-in.-wide strip. Press. Then fold strip in half crosswise and stitch short ends together with a 1/4-in. seam to make a band. Turn band so seam is on inside.

Slip short end of bow through band with folds across bow facing seam of band. Center band along bow. Then slip one end of streamer through band behind bow. Adjust streamers so ends are uneven. Hand-stitch bow and streamers to back of band.

Hand-stitch a 3-in. piece of loop side of Velcro centered across back of bow. Set hook side of Velcro aside.

Cummerbund: Cut a 7-1/2-in.-wide piece of fabric x waist measurement plus 2 in. for outside of cummerbund. Cut a piece of fabric 3-1/2-in.-wide x length of outside of waistband for lining and a same size piece of interfacing.

Center and fuse interfacing to wrong side of lining piece.

Fold outside of cummerbund lengthwise with wrong sides together and edges matching to make a 3-3/4-in.-wide strip. Stitch 2 in. from fold to make a tuck on right side. Open seam. On right side, center fold of tuck along seam. Press new folds along length of cummerbund.

Sew outside and lining of cummerbund together with right sides facing and edges matching, leaving opening for turning. Trim seams and clip corners. Turn right side out. Hand-sew opening

closed. Press.

Cut set-aside Velcro piece in half crosswise. Sew each centered to outside of each end of cummerbund. Bow attaches here.

Hand-sew three hooks and eyes to cummerbund as for waistband.

FINISHING: Thread embroidery needle with pearl cotton. Chain-stitch along fold of all tucks and over visible stitching of tucks on skirt and train, making each stitch about 3/8 in. long. Also chain-stitch over stitching around neck and sleeves of bodice. See Fig. 3 for stitch illustration.

Fig. 3 Chain stitch

Materials Needed (for half-slip):
60-inch-wide white 100% stabilized nylon or nylon tricot—yardage equal to finished length of skirt plus 1-1/2 inches
5 yards of 54-inch-wide white nylon petticoat netting
White all-purpose thread
1 package of 1-inch-wide white elastic

Rotary cutter and mat
Quilter's ruler
Quilter's marking pen or pencil
Standard sewing supplies

Description: Half-slip has elastic waist, center back seam and two ruffles of petticoat netting stitched to right side of slip.

Directions:
Fold one 60-in. edge of slip fabric 1/2 in. to wrong side twice for hem of slip. Machine-stitch close to first fold.

On right side, use quilter's marking pen or pencil to mark a line around slip 12 in. from hem. Mark a second line 23 in. from hem.

Sew selvage edges of slip together with a 1/2-in. seam, leaving 10 in. of seam unstitched above hem. Press seam open.

Press edge opposite hem 1/4 in. to wrong side. Fold 1-1/4 in. again to wrong side to form a channel. Stitch close to first fold, leaving opening for elastic.

Using rotary cutter, cut one 23-in.-wide x 5-yd.-long strip of netting and two 12-in.-wide x 5-yd.-long strips.

Overlap and pin short edges of two 12-in.-wide strips slightly to make one large tube. Gather one edge of tube to fit distance around slip. Pin gathered edge of netting to right side of slip on line 12 in. from hem, matching overlapped edges to sides of slip. Distribute fullness evenly and topstitch netting to slip fabric.

Fold 23-in.-wide strip in half crosswise and mark fold. Fold in half again and mark new folds. Gather and attach strip to line 23 in. from hem of slip.

Insert elastic into channel at waist. Stitch ends together to fit waist. Trim excess elastic. Sew opening closed.

Materials Needed (for headpiece):
3 yards of 54-inch-wide white tulle netting
White all-purpose thread
Fabric scraps from dress—three 5-inch squares, six 4-inch squares and two 3-inch squares
6 inches of 1/2-inch-wide white satin ribbon
3-inch hair comb
White cloth-covered floral wire
White floral tape
1-1/2 yards of 2-inch-wide white sheer ribbon
9 pearl sprays
Quilter's marking pen or pencil
Standard sewing supplies

Finished Size: Headpiece is about 34 inches long.

Directions:
Cut two 54-in. circles of tulle netting.

Place a circle of netting on flat surface. Place second circle on top, leaving 5 in. of bottom circle exposed as shown in Fig. 1. Fold opposite edges of top and bottom circles back, leaving 5 in. exposed as shown in Fig. 2.

Sew a gathering stitch through all lay-

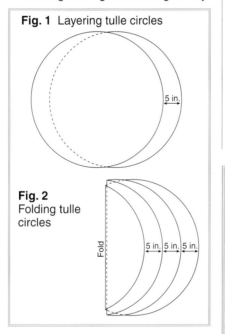

Fig. 1 Layering tulle circles

5 in.

Fig. 2 Folding tulle circles

Fold

5 in. 5 in. 5 in.

ers 1/2 in. from fold. Then add another row 1/4 in. from fold. Draw up threads to make edge along fold about 6 in. long.

Center stitching along the length of 1/2-in.-wide ribbon. Zigzag through all layers, stitching the tulle to the ribbon. Fasten off threads.

Center gathered edge of tulle along straight edge of hair comb with ribbon facing outside curve of comb and hand-stitch to comb.

To make blossoms, fold a 5-in. square of fabric in half crosswise, then fold it in half again to make a 2-1/2-in. square. Use scissors to slightly round edges.

Hold the center of the opened fabric

and twist fabric slightly to make a blossom. Wrap twisted center with white floral tape. Then add a 6-in. piece of white covered floral wire and continue to wrap both until blossom is securely attached to wire. Continue to make blossom picks in this way, using remaining fabric squares. Blossoms need not be identical in shape or size.

Cut sheer ribbon into 6-in.-long pieces. Bring raw edges of each together to make a loop and wrap ends with floral tape. Add a piece of wire to each (as for blossoms) to make ribbon picks.

Place tips of smallest blossoms about 10 in. apart with stems facing each other. Alternate blossom picks, pearl sprays and ribbon picks along stems in desired arrangement, placing largest blossoms in the center. Wrap wire stems together to hold.

Hand-stitch assembled blossoms to gathered edge of tulle and comb of headpiece. ✍

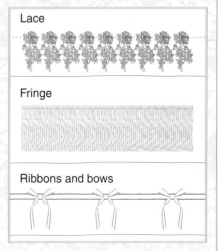

Trim Suggestions

Embellish our design with lace, fringe or ribbons and bows as shown below. Or replace the chain stitching with your choice of trim to create your very own one-of-a-kind dress. The possibilities are endless!

Lace

Fringe

Ribbons and bows

Hats Off to a Western Wedding!

Sherri Aragon (far right) of Fresno, California topped off her Western-style marriage to husband Robert with a cowboy hat trimmed in tasteful tulle, ribbons and silk flowers.

You can quickly achieve the same elegantly casual country look—just be sure to choose hues that go with your bridal party's attire.

Materials Needed:

Cowboy hat—natural straw or color of choice
Two white silk bridal sprays with white roses, rosebuds and pearls
3 yards of tulle netting—dark green or color of choice
1 yard of 1-1/4-inch-wide white iridescent lace
Matching all-purpose thread
Hand-sewing needle
Low-temperature glue gun and glue sticks
Scissors

Finished Size: Bride's hat measures about 15 inches across x 24 inches long, including streamers.

Directions:

Cut a piece of netting 20 in. wide x 3 yds. long. Twist the netting lengthwise so you have a narrow 3-yd.-long strip.

Starting and ending with streamers about 24 in. long at back of hat, wrap netting around crown of hat where it meets the brim. Tie ends in an overhand knot in back. Spot-glue netting to hat.

Place bridal sprays with wire ends facing in opposite directions and flowers meeting in the center. Twist stems to hold them together. Shape stems to match curve of front of hat.

Hand-sew bridal sprays to netting at front of hat as shown in photo at far left. Spot-glue leaves and petals to secure.

Hand-sew center of length of lace to knot at back of hat.

Untwist netting streamers to open. Trim netting and lace to desired length.

Kit Keeps Items at Her Fingertips

Every bride needs a few essentials at her side on her wedding day—whether it's lipstick, blush or even a toothbrush! Which is why Judy Johnson of Missoula, Montana decided to design a bridal survival kit when her friend announced her upcoming nuptials.

Pretty enough to have "in hand" on the big day, the kit has easy-to-access pockets for carrying small necessities.

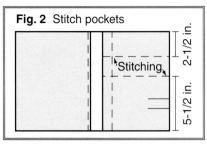

Materials Needed:

Two 10-inch x 16-inch pieces of white satin or fabric to match bridal gown
8-inch x 22-inch piece of white tulle netting
10-inch x 16-inch piece of lightweight quilt batting
One purchased beaded or lace applique for front of kit
1 yard of 3/8-inch-wide white satin ribbon for ties
White all-purpose thread
Standard sewing supplies

Finished Size: Kit measures 9 inches across x 7-1/2 inches high when closed.

Directions:

OUTSIDE: Fold one 10-in. x 16-in. piece of white satin in half with wrong sides together, making an 8-in. x 10-in. rectangle for front of kit. Position applique on right side of rectangle where desired, allowing for 1/2-in. seam allowances. Unfold fabric and hand-sew applique in place, stitching through one thickness of fabric only.

Cut ribbon in half for ties. Center one end of each ribbon on right side of each 10-in. edge of outside of kit with raw edges matching. Baste ribbons in place.

LINING AND POCKETS: Cut white tulle crosswise to make one 8-in. x 10-in. piece and one 8-in. x 12-in. piece for

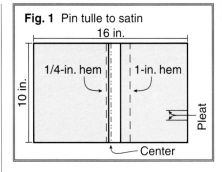

Fig. 1 Pin tulle to satin

16 in.

10 in.

1/4-in. hem   1-in. hem

Pleat

Center

Fig. 2 Stitch pockets

Stitching

2-1/2 in.

5-1/2 in.

pockets of kit.

Sew a 1/4-in. hem along one long edge of 8-in. x 10-in. piece of tulle and a 1-in. hem along one long edge of 8-in. x 12-in. piece of tulle.

Place 10-in.-long hemmed tulle piece right side up on right side of one end of remaining 10-in. x 16-in. piece of white satin. Pin with raw edges matching and hemmed edge facing the center as shown in Fig. 1.

Pin wrong side of 12-in.-long hemmed tulle piece to right side of other end of same piece of satin with raw edges of sides matching and hemmed edge facing the center. To make room for bulky items, pleat edge of tulle opposite hem to fit raw edge of satin as shown in Fig. 1. Baste outside edges of tulle to satin.

Machine-stitch through tulle and satin to make small pockets as shown in Fig. 2.

ASSEMBLY: Place batting on flat surface. Place outside of kit, centered right side up on top of batting. Place lining of kit (piece with tulle pockets) wrong side up, centered on top of outside piece. Pin all three layers together with outside edges matching and ribbon ties sandwiched in between.

Sew layers together with a 1/2-in. seam, leaving an opening for turning. Trim corners. Turn right side out through opening so batting is between layers of satin. Turn raw edges of opening in and hand-stitch opening closed.

Press as needed.

Fold kit in half crosswise and tie ribbons together to close.

Bridal Bag Is Simple to Sew

Can't find a purse to go with your wedding gown? No problem—you can make your own in a fabric and color that matches your dress!

Judy Johnson of Missoula, Montana shares the easy-sew pattern below. She came up with the idea when her daughter was asked to be maid of honor at a friend's wedding.

Materials Needed:
Pattern at right
Tracing paper and pencil
Four 12-inch squares of white satin or fabric to match bridal gown
One purchased beaded or lace applique, sized to fit on front of purse
1 yard of 3/8-inch-wide white satin ribbon for drawstring
1/2 yard of white satin cord for handle
Size 16 embroidery needle
White all-purpose thread
Standard sewing supplies

Finished Size: Purse measures about 10 inches long x 7-1/2 inches across without handle.

Directions:
Use copy machine to enlarge pattern at right to 200%, or mark tracing paper with a 1-in. grid and draw pattern as shown onto tracing paper.

Trace enlarged pattern onto folded tracing paper. Cut out and open for a complete pattern. Cut from fabric as directed on pattern, cutting two pieces for the outside of the purse and two pieces for the lining.

Hand-sew purchased applique to right side of one purse piece 1/2 in. from seamlines for front of purse.

Place the purse front and one lining piece right sides together with raw edges matching. Stitch along straight edge with a 1/4-in. seam. Repeat, using the purse back and lining. Press the seams open.

Pin pieces with right sides of linings together and front and back pieces together, matching seams and outside edges. Sew around outside with a 1/4-in. seam, leaving opening for turning on lining section where indicated on pattern. Turn right side out through opening. Turn the raw edges of the opening in and stitch the opening closed. Slip lining to inside of purse. Press the lining slightly to inside along top seam.

Hand-stitch one end of cord to inside of purse at top of each side seam.

Thread needle with ribbon. For drawstring, hand-stitch ribbon around top of purse with long running stitches, starting and stopping at center front and stitching through outside and lining about 3/4 in. from seam. See Fig. 1 for stitch illustration.

Tie ends of ribbons in an overhand knot. Draw up ribbon to close purse and tie in a bow.

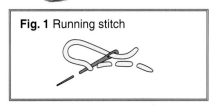

Fig. 1 Running stitch

BRIDAL PURSE PATTERN

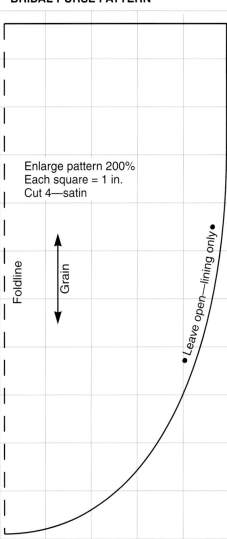

Enlarge pattern 200%
Each square = 1 in.
Cut 4—satin

Foldline

Grain

• Leave open—lining only •

Homegrown Wedding Flowers Are to Have...and to Hold!

Blooming beautiful! That's how guests described Daun and Russ Hembd's on-the-farm wedding in Whitehall, Wisconsin.

"All of the flowers for our wedding were raised on the farm or gathered from the 'back forty'," Daun (at left) details. "After letting them dry, I crafted them into bouquets, boutonnieres, hair wreaths and corsages for the wedding party.

"They're simple to make," she advises. "To save time, you can buy the flowers already dried. You'll have lovely souvenirs of your special day long after the ceremony!"

Materials Needed (for one hair wreath):

Dried materials—several stems each of yarrow and peach statice; straw-flowers—four each of salmon and yellow-gold; baby's breath and green fern or similar dried materials of choice
1/8-inch-wide satin ribbon—4 yards each of off-white and dark coral or two different colors of choice to co-ordinate with flowers
Green floral tape
Green floral wire
20-gauge craft wire
Glue gun and glue sticks
Craft scissors
2-inch-long hair comb

Finished Size: Hair wreath measures about 9 inches across. Ribbons are about 24 inches long.

Directions:
Cut yarrow, statice and baby's breath into sprigs each about 3 in. long.

Wrap a few sprigs each of yarrow, statice and baby's breath together with floral tape to make a small bouquet with a 2-in.-long stem. Make 10 to 12 small bouquets.

Fig. 1a Insert wire through center of flower

Fig. 1b Bend wire

Fig. 1c Pull wire down into flower

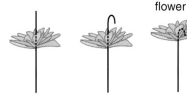

Remove stems of strawflowers and replace natural stems with wire as follows: Cut a piece of floral wire about 4 in. long for each flower. Insert a wire into bottom of each flower and out through top as shown in Fig. 1a. Bend top of each wire as shown in Fig. 1b. Pull wires back down into flowers so wires are hidden as shown in Fig. 1c. Wrap each wire stem with floral tape, adding a bit of green fern to each as you wrap the wire.

Cut a piece of craft wire to fit around the head of the person wearing the hair wreath *plus* 2 in. Wrap entire length of wire with floral tape. Bend 1 in. at each end of wire back onto itself to form a hook. Hook the two ends together and check circle of wire for fit.

Unhook ends and straighten wire. Hold a prepared bouquet to wire so blossom end is even with one hook end and stems point to other end of wire. Wrap stems of bouquet to the wire with floral tape. Place a strawflower over stems of bouquet and wrap stem with floral tape.

Continue to add materials in the same way, alternating colors of straw-flowers and bouquets until entire wire is covered as shown in photo at left.

Hook ends of wire together and check again for fit of hair wreath. Adjust size as needed and then tape over hooked ends to secure.

Cut each color ribbon into three equal lengths. Fold ribbons in half with cut ends matching. Wire ribbons together at fold. Wire ribbons to back of hair wreath over hooked ends. Trim ends of ribbons to desired lengths.

Wire hair comb to inside at front of hair wreath.

Materials Needed (for one brides-maid's bouquet):
Bouquet holder with Styrofoam base (holders are available in bridal section of most craft stores)
Dried materials—several stems each of yarrow and peach statice; strawflowers—five salmon and three yellow-gold; baby's breath and green fern or similar dried materials of choice
1-1/2-inch-wide satin wire-edge rib-bon—3 yards of dark coral or color of choice to coordinate with flowers
1/2 yard of 2-inch-wide pre-gathered off-white lace
Green floral tape

22-gauge green floral wire
Glue gun and glue sticks
Craft scissors

Finished Size: Each bouquet measures about 21 inches long x 12 inches across.

Directions:
Glue the gathered edge of lace to the outside edge of holder. Trim excess lace and discard.

Cut yarrow, statice and baby's breath into sprigs each about 3 in. long.

Wrap two or three sprigs of yarrow and a 6-in. piece of floral wire together with floral tape to make a pick with wire extending beyond stems of yarrow. Insert pick into center of Styrofoam holder. In the same way, make and insert picks of statice, surrounding center yarrow as shown in photo (at far left below).

Remove stems of strawflowers and replace natural stems with wire as follows: Cut a 4-in.-long piece of floral wire for each flower. Insert a wire into bottom of each flower and out through top as shown in Fig. 1a. Bend top of each wire as shown in Fig. 1b. Pull wires back into flowers so wires are hidden as shown in Fig. 1c. Wrap each stem with floral tape.

Insert strawflowers around circle of statice, alternating colors as desired.

Make additional picks of yarrow as before and insert them in a ring around

Fig. 2 Making bow

the previous materials.

Make picks of baby's breath and fern. Add these picks for fill around the outside as shown in photo.

Form ribbon into a large bow with long streamers as shown in Fig. 2. Fasten bow with wire and insert ends of wire into holder at base of center front.

Horseshoe Bouquet Brings Powerful Luck to Couple!

Collette Baker (below) wasn't leaving anything to chance when she wed Michael Van Cleave in Groton, South Dakota. She carried flowers in the shape of a horseshoe to bring them good luck!

Reports mother-of-the-bride Karen Wolter, "Even though she was planning a traditional church wedding, Collette wanted it to have a *country* feeling.

"So I crafted horseshoe-shaped bouquets for her and her bridesmaids using silk flowers and ivy, with a string of miniature lights intertwined.

"I glued the battery pack to the back

of the bouquets…and installed the batteries just before the ceremony so the horseshoes would light up. They were such a hit!"

Materials Needed:
10-inch-diameter Styrofoam circle
Battery-operated light string with 10-12 clear miniature lights (battery pack included)
48 inches of silk ivy garland
Silk flowers—24 ruby red open roses with 1/2-inch to 1-1/2-inch blossoms; 24 miniature sunflowers with 1-1/4-inch blossoms; one bunch of black onion grass; five picks of lavender statice; several sprigs of double white baby's breath
3-inch white felt cowboy hat
Floral wire
Florist pins
Craft scissors or wire cutters
Serrated knife or foam cutter
Low-temperature glue gun and glue sticks

Finished Size: Horseshoe bouquet measures about 12 inches across.

Directions:
Use serrated knife or foam cutter to cut a section from Styrofoam as shown in Fig. 1, making a horseshoe shape.

Wire or glue battery pack to back of horseshoe as shown in Fig. 2.

Wrap ivy garland around horseshoe, covering as much of the inside and outside edges of horseshoe shape and battery pack as possible. Secure garland with florist pins and glue as needed.

String lights along front and sides of horseshoe, coiling excess wiring and spacing lights evenly. Carefully pin and wire lights in place, taking care not to pierce the wiring.

Glue cowboy hat to front of horseshoe as shown in photo below.

Cut roses and sunflowers, leaving stems about 2 in. long. Wrap stems with floral tape. Insert roses around the horseshoe as shown in photo. Then add sunflowers and statice picks, placing them so lights show and foam is covered. Add small sprigs of baby's breath as shown in photo.

Cut individual stems of onion grass. Glue or pin stems between flowers as desired. Loop or curl onion grass and tuck ends in among the flowers.

Fig. 1 Cutting horseshoe shape   **Fig. 2** Attaching battery pack to back

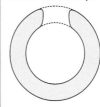

Love Knots Fasten to Rustic Look

Since love is the tie that binds, the homemade bouquets carried by Jennifer Heishman's bridesmaids (see photo below right) for her wedding seemed especially appropriate.

"Swedish love knots are supposed to bring the bride and groom good luck," confides Jennifer's aunt, Jane Jenkins of Baltimore, Maryland. "My sister-in-law, Robin Stultz, made them from baler twine and trimmed them with silk flowers. They were the perfect accent for the Western-style bridal gown I designed."

Jennifer and Jeremy Haviland tied the knot in front of her great-grandfather's barn in Criders, Virginia.

Materials Needed:
1-1/2-inch-high x 1/4-inch-thick wooden heart
Acrylic craft paint—blue or color of choice
Small paintbrush
3-1/2 yards of 1/4-inch-diameter 3-ply natural twine rope or braided baler twine
16-inch square of heavy cardboard
Five sprigs of silk fern or other greens
1/2 yard of 4mm white string pearls
Silk flowers—five 3/4-inch dark red rosebuds and three white daisy picks with several 1/2-inch blossoms or similar flowers in colors of choice

Several sprigs of baby's breath
1-1/2 yards each of 1/4-inch-wide light blue satin picot ribbon and 1/8-inch-wide dark blue satin ribbon or ribbons in two coordinating colors of choice
Straight pins
Glue gun and glue sticks
Scissors

Finished Size: Love knot measures about 15 inches long x 11 inches across.

Directions:
Paint all sides of wooden heart blue. Let dry.

Place cardboard on a flat surface and keep pins handy to secure rope as you form the love knot. Mark the center of the cardboard.

Cut twine rope in half. Pin one end of a rope half to the center of the cardboard. Form rope into a love knot, following the direction of the arrows for that half of rope as shown in Fig. 1.

Repeat with other half of rope, following direction of other set of arrows to make an intertwining love knot.

Spot-glue ropes together to secure, keeping love knot flat and taking care not to glue love knot to cardboard. Let dry. Remove love knot from cardboard.

Tie ends of ropes in overhand knots, leaving each rope end about 8 in. long. Trim ends of ropes close to knot.

Glue stems of greens to the center of the love knot, fanning tips out between the loops.

Cut string pearls into three pieces of equal length. Glue ends of each length together to form a loop. Glue ends to center of love knot so loops of pearls are inside a loop of the love knot.

Glue baby's breath, daises and rosebuds to the center of the love knot as shown in the photo at left.

Working with light and dark blue ribbons as one, tie ribbons into a multi-loop bow measuring about 4 in. across. Glue bow to love knot below flowers as shown in photo. Trim ends of ribbons to desired length.

Glue heart to loop of love knot as shown in photo.

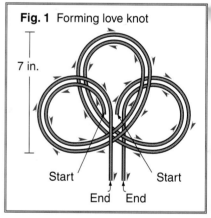

Fig. 1 Forming love knot

7 in.

Start   Start
End   End

Bouquet Blooms with Sentiment

Country romance was as near as Serena Verboom's creative fingertips when she designed her own wedding gown and heart-shaped bouquet.

From Providence Bay, Ontario, the wife of Marius, a farmer, (see pair at right) writes, "I wanted a traditional cascade bouquet, but I couldn't find a holder I liked.

"When I saw a heart-shaped mat in a craft shop, I knew it was time to improvise! Silk roses and a bit of lace added the romantic touches I was looking for."

Materials Needed:

12-inch natural rattan heart mat (available at most craft stores)
Bouquet holder with Styrofoam base (available in bridal sections of most craft stores)
One purchased white silk rose bridal cascade
Silk flowers—three each of burgundy and blue open roses with 2-inch-wide blossoms, six burgundy open roses with 1-inch-wide blossoms, four blue open roses with 1-inch-wide blossoms, one 1-inch-long blue rosebud and five sprigs of burgundy statice or similar flowers in colors of choice
24 green silk rose leaves
1 yard of 1-1/2-inch-wide pre-gathered white lace
Floral tape
Floral wire
1/8-inch-wide satin picot ribbon—3 yards each of light blue and rose or two different colors of choice to co-ordinate with flowers
3 yards of 3mm white string pearls
Glue gun and glue sticks
Wire cutters
Scissors

Finished Size: Bouquet measures about 30 inches long x 12 inches across.

Directions:

Make a horizontal slit across the center of the rattan heart for handle of cascade holder. Insert handle of holder through slit from front to back. Glue or wire holder into place.

Glue pre-gathered lace to front of heart shape, leaving about 1 in. of the rattan showing. Trim excess lace.

Insert stem of rose cascade into foam of holder with flowers extending beyond point of rattan heart.

Cut burgundy and blue roses and blue rosebud from stems, leaving 3-in. to 4-in.-long stems on blossoms. Add roses to cascade by wrapping the cut stems around stems of flowers in the cascade. Alternate sizes and colors of flowers as shown in photo below. Add blue rosebud to bottom of cascade. Wrap stems with floral tape to cover wires.

Add green silk rose leaves and sprigs of statice randomly to cascade as desired. Glue or wire stems to secure.

Cut two 6-in.-long pieces of each color of ribbon. Fold ribbons in half and wrap ends of each together to make picks. Insert ribbon picks into holder around center flowers.

Working with ribbons and pearl string as one, wrap ribbons and pearl string into several 18-in.-long loops. Wrap one end of loops with craft wire to hold and twist ends of wire together to make a pick. Insert ribbon and pearl pick into foam base so loops hang down from flower cascade.

She Roped in Western-Style Accents for Wedding

You can easily tie a bunch of these bloomers into your country nuptials—they're "knot" a problem at all to make!

Jeanna Tucker (at right) of Waterloo, Indiana fashioned the bright bridal accents after the pastime she and husband Bill share. "We like to compete in local rodeos," she happily acknowledges.

"Crafting with rope seemed appropriate. The small circles made nice boutonnieres and corsages, while the larger ones were used as bridesmaids' bouquets and pew trims at church."

Materials Needed (for each bridesmaid's bouquet or pew trim):

66 inches of 1/4-inch-diameter 3-ply natural jute rope
Silk flowers—one spray with several 1-1/2-inch-wide teal blossoms and three sprays with several 1/2-inch-wide white blossoms or similar flowers in colors of choice
1/4-inch-wide satin ribbon—1 yard each of teal and white or two different colors of choice to coordinate with flowers
Craft wire
Glue gun and glue sticks
Wire cutters
Scissors

Finished Size: Bridesmaid's bouquet or pew trim measures about 18 inches long x 12 inches wide.

Directions:

Working on a flat surface and starting and stopping on the left side, coil jute rope to make a flat 12-in.-long oval as shown in Fig. 1. Spot-glue ropes together where they are touching, keeping oval flat.

Arrange flowers in your hand. When you are pleased with the arrangement, wire them to the left side of the coiled rope, covering the rope ends. Trim ends of flower stems close to wire.

Working with both colors of satin ribbon as one, wrap ribbons over wire. Tie ribbons in bow if desired.

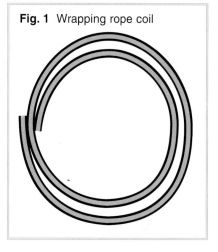

Fig. 1 Wrapping rope coil

Materials Needed (for each boutonniere):

Silk flower spray with six 3/4-inch-wide teal blossoms or similar flowers in color of choice
Silk rose leaf
24 inches of 3-ply jute string
Baby's breath
One beardless wheat head
Glue gun and glue sticks
Scissors
Corsage pin

Finished Size: Boutonniere is about 3-1/2 inches long x 2-3/4 inches wide.

Directions:

Starting and stopping at the bottom, coil jute string to make a flat oval measuring about 3-1/4 in. long x 2-3/4 in.

wide as shown in Fig. 1. Glue ends of jute string and loops together at the bottom only. Trim excess jute string.

Glue leaf to base of coil. Glue wheat head to leaf and baby's breath around wheat head. Cut teal blossoms from spray, varying length of stems. Glue blossoms in desired arrangement.

You can also make a wedding corsage by coiling 27 in. of jute string as shown in Fig. 1, making a flat coil about 4 in. long x 3-1/2 in. wide.

Glue loops together as for boutonniere. Add your choice of flowers in desired arrangement to coordinate with wedding colors or attire.

Insert corsage pin through base of jute coil to attach boutonniere or corsage to garment.

Fig. 1 Wrapping jute string coil

Bridesmaids Held Hats in Hand

Uncapping a country-fresh way to carry flowers down the aisle is what Becky Bair-Davis (above) did when she embellished simple felt cowboy hats for her bridal attendants.

"My mother and I circled the brims with blossoms and ribbons," briefs the Fletcher, Ohio farm wife. The bedecked Stetsons also helped brighten the reception, where they were displayed on hat stands around the hall.

Materials Needed (for each):
Cowboy hat—black felt or color of choice
Silk flowers—three each of teal and white roses with 2-inch-long buds, six navy open roses with 1-inch-wide blossoms, four burgundy open roses with 1-inch-wide blossoms, six burgundy rosebuds, three navy rosebuds and five small white flower picks or similar flowers in colors of choice
Baby's breath
Satin ribbon—6 yards of 1/8-inch-wide white and 3 yards each of 1/4-inch-wide teal, 1/8-inch-wide navy and 1/16-inch-wide burgundy or ribbons in colors of choice to coordinate with flowers
2-1/4 yards of 3mm iridescent string pearls
Glue gun and glue sticks
Scissors
Wire cutters

Finished Size: Hat measures about 15 inches across x 28 inches long, including streamers.

Directions:
Cut all roses, rosebuds and leaves from stems, trimming close to the base of each. Starting and stopping about 2 in. from center back, glue roses to the hat where the crown meets the brim. Alternate colors and sizes of roses as shown in the photo above.

Glue rosebuds between roses, alternating colors as before. Then glue baby's breath, leaves and white flower picks around the outer edge as shown in the photo.

Cut teal, navy and burgundy ribbons into two equal lengths. Cut white ribbon into four equal lengths. Working with all ribbons as one, tie ribbons into a bow measuring about 7 in. across. Glue bow to center back of hat between flowers.

Cut string pearls into five equal lengths. Glue one end of each length to center back of hat under bow.

Trim ribbons and string pearl streamers to desired length.

Her Well-Heeled Holder's In Step with Bridal Diners

Keeping pace with hungry reception guests as they mosey through a tasty buffet is easy—when you corral flatware and napkins into simple cowboy boot containers!

Jan Arndt of Washington, Illinois assembled the quick plastic canvas helpers for her daughter Jenifer's marriage to Butch Ludwig. "Since she's a barrel racer, I thought the boots were a perfect touch," notes the proud mom.

"Not only were they easy to carry, the holders made nice mementos for guests to take home with them."

Materials Needed (for each):
Charts at right
7-count plastic canvas—one 10-1/2-inch x 13-1/2-inch sheet of red or color of choice
Plastic canvas yarn—white or color of choice
Plastic canvas needle
Small metal star and silver bead or other decorative trims
Low-temperature glue gun and glue sticks
Scissors
Napkin and silverware

Finished Size: Holder measures 5-3/4 inches tall x 4-1/2 inches across.

Directions:
Making sure to count the bars and not the holes, cut one piece of plastic canvas according to chart A for the back of the boot. Cut another piece of plastic canvas according to chart B for the front of the boot.

Cut a 60-in. length of yarn so you can do all stitching with one length of yarn. Do not knot the yarn. Instead, leave a tail of yarn on the back and work the first few stitches over it. To end yarn, run yarn under last few stitches on back and clip yarn close to work. Refer to Fig. 1 for stitch illustrations.

Overcast top edge of front boot only. Do not end yarn.

Place front of boot on top of the back of the boot with foot portions of boots matching. With same length of yarn, whipstitch boots together along the side and bottom edges where they are layered. Then overcast around the single layer of top of the back boot. End yarn.

Glue star and bead trims to front of holder where desired.

Wrap napkin around silverware and insert into opening of boot as shown in photo at right.

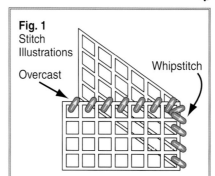

Fig. 1
Stitch Illustrations
Overcast
Whipstitch

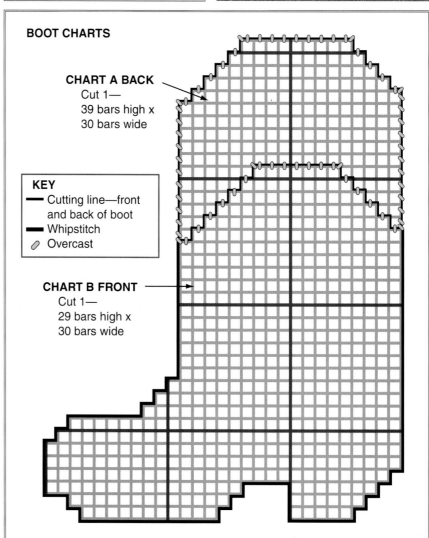

BOOT CHARTS

CHART A BACK
Cut 1—
39 bars high x
30 bars wide

KEY
— Cutting line—front and back of boot
▬ Whipstitch
⬭ Overcast

CHART B FRONT
Cut 1—
29 bars high x
30 bars wide

Guests Will Savor Flower Favors

Offer these rosebuds at your home-grown wedding fete…and watch sweet smiles crop up all over!

The pleasing posies from Deb Henderson of Maroa, Illinois are well rooted in tastiness. "To create them, I used chocolate candy kisses," Deb reveals. "They were easy to put together and a hit on our special day."

She suggests making lots of roses and arranging them in a flat flower basket…as if you had just picked them from your garden. Use them as table favors, or hand them out when folks sign the guest book.

Materials Needed (for each):
Two candy kisses—with silver, red or red-and-silver striped wrapper
One hard candy with pink or red wrapper
5-inch square of red cellophane or plastic wrap
2-inch x 4-inch piece of green metallic tissue paper
8-inch length of 16-gauge floral stem wire
Green floral tape
Double-stick tape

Finished Size: Each candy rose is 10-1/2 inches tall x 2 inches across.

Directions:
Use small piece of double-stick tape to hold the bottoms of two candy kisses together as shown in Fig. 1.

Center square of red cellophane or plastic wrap on tip of one candy kiss. Wrap the two candy kisses, covering them to resemble a rosebud. Twist the cellophane or plastic wrap at the tip of the other candy kiss.

Insert floral wire into twist of cellophane or plastic wrap. Tape twist of cellophane or plastic wrap securely with floral tape. Continue to wrap floral wire for about 2 in.

Tape one end of paper wrapper of hard candy to floral wire and continue wrapping stem for another 2 in.

Pleat green metallic tissue paper diagonally to make leaf as shown in Fig. 2. Tape leaf to wire and continue to wrap remainder of wire with floral tape.

Fig. 1 Tape candy kisses together

Fig. 2 Pleat green metallic tissue paper

Rope Pin Wraps Finery in Twine Fashion…

Stringing together a Western-style accent for groomsmen to don is a cinch, thanks to the wrangler boutonniere Jennifer Bradshaw from Leadville, Colorado shares here!

"All it takes is some cord, a mini cowboy hat and a few other simple supplies," she outlines of the design she dreamed up for her down-home "I do's".

"This hearty two-loop one is what my husband wore. I also fixed single loop versions for the rest of the fellows."

Materials Needed:
22 inches of natural macrame cord or jute twine
2-inch square of red bandanna fabric
or other fabric of choice
2-inch felt cowboy hat—black or color of choice
Dried materials—sprig each of baby's breath and prairie grass or other dried materials of choice
Glue gun and glue sticks
Scissors
Corsage pin

Finished Size: Boutonniere is about 4 inches high x 3 inches across.

Directions:
Cut one piece of macrame cord or jute twine 10 in. long and another 12 in. long.

Tie a knot close to both ends of each length of cord.

Loop each cord as shown in Fig. 1. Glue to hold where cords overlap.

Place one cord on top of the other so loops overlap to make a heart shape as shown in Fig. 2. Glue cords where they are touching to hold. Let dry.

Glue prairie grass and baby's breath to base of loops.

Fold square of bandanna fabric in half diagonally with wrong sides together to form a triangle. Make a 1/4-in. pleat centered along fold of fabric. Glue pleat to hold. Glue fabric to cords at base of heart as shown in photo above.

Glue hat to heart as shown in photo. Use corsage pin to attach boutonniere to groom's or groomsmen's shirts.

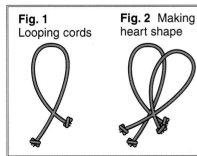

Fig. 1 Looping cords

Fig. 2 Making heart shape

Blue Jean Accent Pockets Pretty Look for Pew

To mark the occasion of her son's wedding, Margaret Byron of La Grande, Oregon promptly got the "blues"—with very happy results! This proud mother cleverly constructed pew decorations using pockets she cut from old blue jeans.

"Brad's bride, Carol, showed me a similar pocket trim a friend had made," details Margaret. "From that, I got the idea to fix up a cowboy version featuring a hat, lasso, bandanna and flowers."

Notes daughter-in-law Carol, "The pockets came in handy afterward, too. We gave them to friends who helped with our special celebration."

Materials Needed:

Pair of old denim jeans
Bandanna—burgundy or color of choice
Silk flowers—two burgundy open roses with 1-1/2-inch blossoms, three burgundy rosebuds with 1-inch-long buds and three off-white open roses with 1-inch blossoms or similar flowers in colors of choice
Dried materials—several sprigs each of white statice, white baby's breath, miniature ivy and burgundy flowers or other dried materials to coordinate with your choice of flowers
1-1/2 yards of 3-ply jute string
3-inch cowboy hat—black or color of choice
Wire coat hanger
Wire cutters
Glue gun and glue sticks
Scissors
Pencil

Finished Size: Pocket pew marker is about 7 inches across x 11-1/2 inches high.

Directions:

Carefully cut a back pocket from jeans, cutting as close as possible to outside edge of pocket. Trim any stray threads.

Use wire cutters to cut a 20-in. piece of wire from coat hanger. Wrap wire around pencil, starting about 6 in. from one end. Bend wire for handle as shown in photo above left. Insert ends of wire into pocket with top of curve about 6 in. from top edge of pocket. Glue ends of wire inside pocket to secure.

Fold bandanna in half diagonally to make a triangle. Cut a corner from bandanna as shown in Fig. 1. Set corner piece aside. Then cut bandanna in half along diagonal fold.

Tuck cut edge of one bandanna half inside pocket opening, leaving tip of corner about 1 in. from wire as shown in photo. Glue cut edge to inside back of pocket, taking care not to glue pocket shut.

Cut silk flowers and dried materials, leaving stems about 3 in. long. Glue stems of burgundy and off-white roses inside pocket as shown in photo. Add statice, baby's breath, miniature ivy and burgundy flowers to fill in open spaces.

Cut 18 in. of jute string. Tie piece in a bow around coil of wire as shown in photo.

Coil remaining jute string, leaving a 6-in. tail. Glue jute string to front of pocket where shown in photo.

Glue reserved corner piece of bandanna to underside of brim of hat and a small sprig of burgundy flowers to outside brim of hat.

Glue hat over tail of jute string as shown in photo.

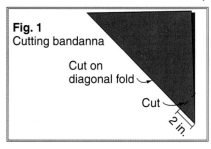

Fig. 1
Cutting bandanna

Cut on diagonal fold

Cut

2 in.

Rope Wreath Enhances Benches

Taking a cue from son Brad's cowboy ways, Margaret Byron lassoed another aisle accent for his wedding in record time.

Describes the mother of the groom, "Brad's a calf roper and had plenty of used piggin' strings around. I simply coiled some up and added horseshoes, flowers and mini cowboy hats.

"We placed the wreaths on the ends of the church pews. They were a big hit!"

Materials Needed:

6 feet of piggin' string (calf roping rope)
or other stiff rope
1 pony size horseshoe
1-1/2 yards of 2-1/2-inch-wide paper lace ribbon—ecru or color of choice
Silk flowers—four burgundy open roses with 1-1/2-inch blossoms and five burgundy rosebuds with 1-inch-long buds or similar flowers in colors of choice
Dried materials—six bearded wheat heads, white statice, white baby's breath, miniature ivy and small burgundy flowers or other dried materials to coordinate with your choice of flowers

3-inch felt cowboy hat—white or color of choice
Three 1/2-inch ribbon roses—burgundy or color of choice
12 inches of 3-ply jute string
Craft wire
Wire cutters
Scissors
Glue gun and glue sticks

Finished Size: Rope pew marker measures about 12 inches across.

Directions:
Coil piggin' string or rope into circle about 9-1/2 in. across and secure with craft wire where shown in Fig. 1.

Glue ivy or other greens to top of rope over wire with stems pointing toward center. Wire as needed to secure. Add statice and wheat heads to each side. Then add rosebuds and rose blossoms. Fill in with remaining materials, leaving center of arrangement open for placement of bow.

Form ribbon into a multi-loop bow as shown in Fig. 2. Wire bow to center of arrangement as shown in photo below left.

Wire horseshoe to side of rope where shown in photo. Glue hat and a bit of statice to horseshoe, covering wire.

Form jute string into a 2-in. coil. Referring to photo for placement, glue coil, ribbon roses and a bit of greenery to brim of hat.

Cut a 6-in. piece of craft wire. Attach wire to back of pew marker behind the bow for a hanging loop.

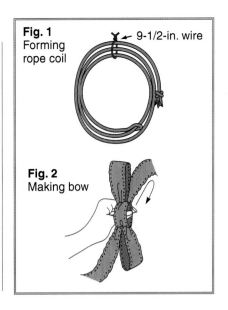

Fig. 1 Forming rope coil

←9-1/2-in. wire

Fig. 2 Making bow

Bow Brings Style to Aisle

Here's an easy idea that will let you unwind—even in the midst of hectic wedding preparations!

Sandi Rawie of Silverton, Oregon shares the quick-to-craft pew adornment she and daughter Krista created from paper twist and raffia for Krista's outdoor nuptials (see photo below right).

"We wanted the trimmings to be fuss-free," elaborates Sandi. "This bow is a fine example. It takes only minutes to make!"

Materials Needed:
3 yards of 4-inch-wide or 5-inch-wide paper twist—rose or color of choice
15 to 20 strands of natural raffia
Craft wire
Wire cutters
Scissors

Finished Size: Paper twist bow measures about 20 inches long x 12 inches across.

Directions:
Untwist paper twist. Form paper twist into a bow as shown in Fig. 1, making three loops on each side and leaving 18-in.-long streamers. Wire center of bow to secure it.

Working with all strands of raffia as one, tie raffia into a bow a bit smaller than the paper twist bow. Wire raffia bow to center front of paper twist bow.

Cut a piece of wire 6 in. long. Wire ends to back of bow for a hanging loop.

Cut ends of streamers as shown in photo at right. Trim raffia to desired length.

Fig. 1 Forming paper twist bow

Keenan Photography, Silverton, Ore.

His'n'Hers Markers Let Guests Take Sides

When it came to simplifying seating at her daughter's wedding service, Shirley Hodowanec of Birdsboro, Pennsylvania took the matter in stride by uncovering an eye-catching decorating scheme.

"I brightened pews on one side of the aisle with lacy parasols trimmed with white boots, then lined the other side with black-boot versions," she reveals.

"As guests arrived at the church, they could tell that white meant 'bride' and black meant 'groom' and happily moved to the right section to watch Tanya and Mike Morret (below) exchange vows."

The footwear can serve in other ways as well. "You can also use them for favors or place markers," suggests Shirley.

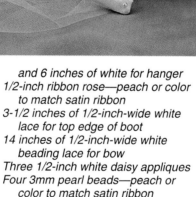

Materials Needed (for each boot):
Pattern on next page
Tracing paper and pencil
Polyester stuffing
Standard sewing supplies
12-inch purchased white lace parasol (available in bridal section of most craft stores)
4 inches of green and white silk ivy garland
3 yards of 6-inch-wide white tulle netting
1 yard of 4mm white string pearls
Low-temperature glue gun and glue sticks

Additional Materials Needed (for lady's boot):
7-inch x 12-inch piece of white satin
Matching all-purpose thread
10-1/2 inches of 3mm white string pearls
1/8-inch-wide satin ribbon—14 inches of peach or color of choice for bow
and 6 inches of white for hanger
1/2-inch ribbon rose—peach or color to match satin ribbon
3-1/2 inches of 1/2-inch-wide white lace for top edge of boot
14 inches of 1/2-inch-wide white beading lace for bow
Three 1/2-inch white daisy appliques
Four 3mm pearl beads—peach or color to match satin ribbon

Additional Materials Needed (for man's boot):
7-inch x 12-inch piece of black satin
Matching all-purpose thread
6 inches of 1/4-inch-wide black satin ribbon for hanger
3/4-inch gold star charm or bead for spur

Finished Size: Each parasol pew marker is about 18 inches long x 12 inches across.

Directions:
FOR EACH: Trace pattern at right onto tracing paper and cut out. For each boot, cut two from same color satin as directed on pattern.

Pin two matching boot pieces with right sides together and edges matching. Stitch around boot with 1/4-in. seam where shown on pattern, leaving opening where indicated on man's boot for star spur. Clip corners and curves.

Turn boot right side out through top opening. Press as needed. Stuff firmly with polyester stuffing.

Turn top unstitched edge of boot 1/4

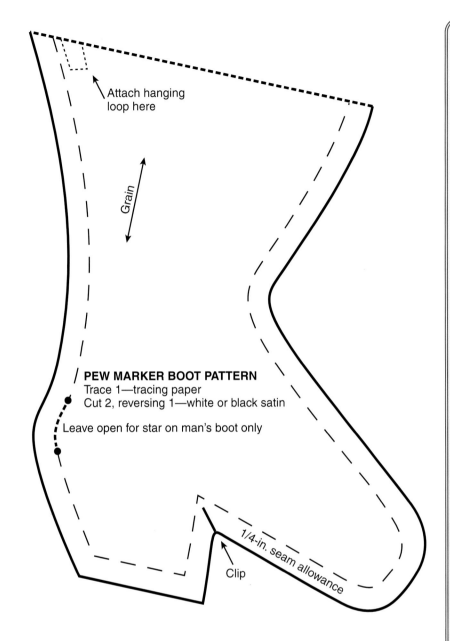

PEW MARKER BOOT PATTERN
Trace 1—tracing paper
Cut 2, reversing 1—white or black satin

Leave open for star on man's boot only

Attach hanging loop here

Grain

1/4-in. seam allowance

Clip

in. to wrong side. Fold matching ribbon for hanging loop in half and stitch ends together. Pin ends of loop to top of boot where shown on pattern. Hand-sew opening closed, catching ends of hanger in stitching.

Open parasol and glue string pearls to gathered edge of lace on parasol. Trim the excess.

Glue ivy to top of the parasol as shown in photo above left.

Cut tulle netting into two pieces of equal length. Working with both pieces as one, tie netting into a large bow with 18-in.-long streamers. Glue bow to one side of ivy at top of parasol.

FINISHING: Lady's Boot: Glue 3-1/2-in. piece of lace to top edge of white boot. Trim excess.

Tie beading lace into a small bow. Glue bow to top of boot over lace.

Tie peach ribbon into a small multi-loop bow. Glue bow to center of beading lace bow. Thread streamers of ribbon bow through openings of beading lace streamers. Trim ends to desired length.

Glue string pearls around ankle of boot as shown in photo. Trim excess. Glue center of remaining string pearls to center of ribbon bow.

Glue ribbon rose to center of bow and daisies to heel of boot as shown in photo. Glue a peach bead to the center of each daisy and to tip of boot. Glue hanging loop of boot to top of parasol.

Man's Boot: Glue star into heel opening of black boot for spur. Glue hanging loop of boot to top of parasol.

Cut an 18-in.-wide x 84-in.-long strip of tulle netting. Form tulle netting into a large bow with 14-in.-long streamers as shown in Fig. 2.

Center the tulle bow on the back of the rope as shown in photo. Wire the bow to rope to secure.

Center gold ribbon on top of length of pink ribbon. Working with both ribbons as one, tie the ribbons into a small multi-loop bow with 12-in.-long streamers as shown in Fig. 3.

Wire or glue ribbon bow to front as shown in photo, concealing the stems of the flowers.

Shape ends of rope and tulle bow as shown in photo. Trim tulle netting and ribbon ends to desired length.

Wire plastic bow clip to back. Or form a hanging loop from craft wire and attach hanging loop to back of pew marker.

Spray pew marker with gold glitter spray if desired. Let dry.

Ease Is Tied into Church Trim

Harnessing a fast way to festoon pews for rural "I do's" is this beautiful bow. Bride Jennifer Vaith, whose horseshoe candle holders grace the opposite page, shares the instructions for the bow below.

"My mother, Barbara Ulmer, deserves all the credit for this trim. She created the bows by dressing up plain rope with tulle and silk blooms," says Jennifer, from Menno, South Dakota.

"After the ceremony, we brought the bows to the reception to add to the decor there."

Materials Needed:
4 feet of 1/2-inch-diameter 3-ply tan nylon rope
2-1/3 yards of off-white tulle netting
Silk flowers—burgundy spray with three 1-1/2-inch blossoms and burgundy pick with four 1/2-inch blossoms or flowers in color of choice
1/4-inch-wide ribbon—2 yards each of gold metallic and pink or colors of
choice to coordinate with flowers
6 inches of silk ivy garland
Floral tape
Craft wire
Wire cutters
Glue gun and glue sticks
Purchased plastic bow or pew clip (optional)
Gold glitter spray (optional)

Finished Size: Pew marker is about 12 inches across x 20 inches long.

Directions:
Glue plies of rope together at each end or singe ends to prevent raveling.

Form rope into two loops as shown in Fig. 1. Glue or wire rope at intersection to secure.

Glue ivy to front of rope with leaves pointing down toward ends of rope as shown in photo above. Glue floral spray to front with flowers pointing up. Remove flowers from pick, leaving a short stem on each. Use floral tape to attach flowers along stem of ivy as shown in photo.

Fig. 1 Forming rope loops

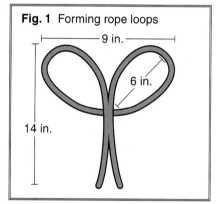

9 in.

6 in.

14 in.

Fig. 2 Making tulle bow

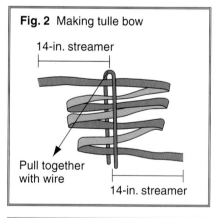

14-in. streamer

Pull together with wire

14-in. streamer

Fig. 3 Making multi-loop bow

Golden Holders Are in Step With Her Down-Home Hitchin'

To give her wedding country flair, Jennifer Vaith of Menno, South Dakota didn't hesitate to horse around.

"Since Dean and I are active in the local saddle club, we decided to tie our decorations into riding," she smiles. "We also wanted to keep costs down, which meant making things ourselves. Luckily, we got plenty of help from our families."

The candle holders that brightened her reception are a prime example of some of the "horse sense" Jennifer and her clan relied on.

"Dean and my brother welded the horseshoes to form holders, then I painted them and my mom created the flower accents," Jennifer sums up. "They were inexpensive and attractive, too!"

Materials Needed (for each):
Welder and welding supplies
Gold spray paint
Floral tape
Wire cutters

Materials Needed (for upside-down horseshoe candle holder, with horseshoe tips pointing down):
Two 000PL size horseshoes
12-inch candle—white or color of choice
3/4-inch length of 3/4-inch-diameter conduit pipe or diameter to fit base of candle
Silk flowers—five burgundy flowers with 1-1/2-inch blossoms and three white flowers with 1/2-inch to 1-inch blossoms or similar flowers in colors of choice
18 inches of silk ivy garland

Materials Needed (for right-side-up horseshoe candle holder, with horseshoe tips pointing up):
Two 00PL size horseshoes
3-inch square of 3/16-inch-thick metal
Purchased 1-1/4-inch ivy climber with
pink and burgundy flowers or assorted pink and burgundy silk flowers and 12 inches of silk ivy garland
Purchased plastic candle holder with flat bottom
12-inch candle—burgundy or color of choice
Glue gun and glue sticks or floral adhesive

Finished Size: Each candle holder measures about 3-1/2 inches across x 5 inches tall without candle.

Directions:
WELDING: For upside-down horseshoe candle holder, weld side of pipe to flat side of rounded portion of one horseshoe. In the same way, weld another horseshoe to opposite side of pipe so horseshoes stand level. See Fig. 1.

For right-side-up horseshoe candle holder, weld edge of metal square to flat side of rounded portion of one horseshoe so horseshoe stands upright as shown in photo at right and metal square sits flat. Weld another horseshoe to opposite side of metal square in the same way. See Fig. 2.

PAINTING: When candle holders are thoroughly cooled, spray-paint all surfaces gold. Apply additional coats as needed for complete coverage, allowing drying time between each coat. Let dry.

FINISHING: Upside-Down Horseshoe Candle Holder: Insert a candle into opening of pipe.

Cut burgundy and white flowers, leaving a short stem on each. Use floral tape to attach flowers to ivy garland, alternating the colors and sizes of the flowers as desired.

Wrap one end of ivy garland around base of candle and continue to wrap remaining ivy in a spiral around candle as shown in photo above left.

Right-Side-Up Horseshoe Candle Holder: Use glue or floral adhesive to attach flat bottom of purchased plastic candle holder to center of metal square.

Insert candle into plastic holder.

Slip circle of floral climber over candle and into clips on plastic candle holder. Wrap remaining climber in a spiral around candle as shown.

If making your own climber, cut pink and burgundy flowers, leaving a short stem on each. Use floral tape to attach

flowers to ivy garland, alternating colors and sizes of flowers as desired.

Wrap one end of the ivy garland around the base of plastic candle holder and glue to secure. Continue to wrap remaining ivy around the candle as shown in the photo above.

Fig. 1 Welding upside-down horseshoe candle holder

Fig. 2 Welding right-side-up horseshoe candle holder

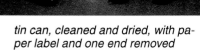

tin can, cleaned and dried, with paper label and one end removed

Tin Trims Tap into Bright Look

The flame of love burned bright at the wedding of Billie Jo and Dave Pacifico (above right). It did the same at the reception, thanks to clever candle holders crafted by the bride's mom, Georganne Burgess of New Castle, Pennsylvania.

"Using clean tin cans, I punched loving designs in each, then placed votives inside," Georganne says. "The holders added real shine to the tables."

Materials Needed (for one candle holder):
Patterns below
Tracing paper and pencil
Masking tape
Votive or tea candle
Finishing nails
Hammer
Spray paint—silver or other color of choice
One 14-1/2-ounce to 16-ounce empty

Finished Size: Each candle holder is about 3-1/4 inches across x 4-1/4 inches tall.

Directions:
Trace patterns below onto tracing paper.

Center and tape each pattern onto opposite sides of the tin can to create designs as shown in photo above left.

Punch the designs, using a nail and hammer, moving from dot to dot. Remove the patterns.

Spray outside of can with silver paint. Let dry.

Place votive or tea candle inside can.

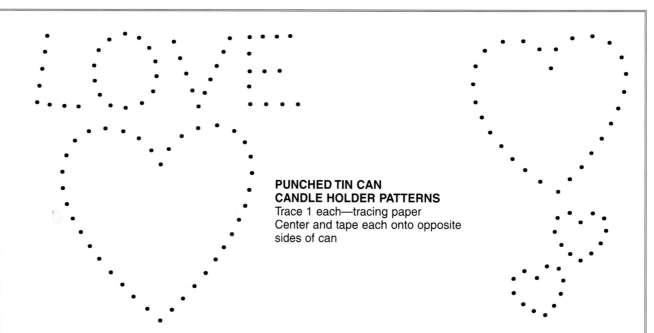

**PUNCHED TIN CAN
CANDLE HOLDER PATTERNS**
Trace 1 each—tracing paper
Center and tape each onto opposite
sides of can

Table Decor's in the Bag With Flower-Filled Sacks

To field this rustic centerpiece, mother-of-the-groom Julie Johnston simply took stock of her surroundings.

"Feed sacks are such a common sight in our rural area, I thought it would be fun to incorporate them into decorations for our son Leon's country wedding," she pens from Shaunavon, Saskatchewan.

"First, I stitched scaled-down bags from burlap, then stiffened them and tucked dried blooms inside. We placed one on each table at the celebration.

"They were easy," concludes Julie, "and very appropriate!"

Materials Needed (for one burlap centerpiece):
15-inch x 12-inch piece of natural burlap
Matching all-purpose thread
26 inches of 1/4-inch-wide satin ribbon—red or color of choice
1-inch wooden heart
Acrylic craft paint—dark green or color of choice
Small flat paintbrush
Floral foam
1 cup of sand or aquarium gravel in small plastic bag (used to weight arrangement and make it stable)
Nine dried red roses or other flowers in color of choice
Several stems each of eucalyptus and

baby's breath for filler
White glue or commercial fabric stiffener
Waxed paper
Craft scissors
Glue gun and glue sticks
Standard sewing supplies

Finished Size: Burlap centerpiece is about 12 inches high x 7 inches across. Finished size may vary depending on final shape of container and materials used for arrangement.

Directions:
Paint all sides of heart desired color. Let dry.

Fold burlap in half crosswise with raw edges matching, making a 7-1/2-in. x 12-in. rectangle. Machine-stitch with a 1/2-in. seam along one 7-1/2-in. edge and along 12-in. edge. Turn right side out. Fold down top edge about 1-1/2 in. to outside. Trim exposed seam to 1/4 in.

Dilute glue with a few drops of water, making it thin enough to soak into burlap. Saturate burlap bag with thinned glue. Flatten to squeeze out excess thinned glue and smooth burlap. Or apply commercial fabric stiffener to burlap bag following manufacturer's directions.

While burlap bag is still wet, place weighted plastic bag into bottom of sack. Then stuff sack with crumpled waxed paper and shape sack as desired, mak-

ing sure bottom is flat and bag stands alone. Set on waxed paper to dry.

Wrap ribbon around top of sack and tie ends in a small bow as shown in photo above. Spot-glue ribbon to secure. Glue heart beneath bow.

Remove crumpled waxed paper from sack. Cut floral foam to fit and place foam inside sack.

Add dried flowers, eucalyptus and baby's breath to make arrangement as desired.

This Hat Has Bridal Favors Covered

Want to round up a wedding favor country folks will appreciate? Set your cap for this simple straw hat—it has tasty treats tucked under its brim!

Lori Yarish of Danville, Pennsylvania came up with the idea for her wedding and reports that the tulle-covered token is quick to craft. "Even better, it was a big hit at the reception," she offers.

Materials Needed:
4-1/2-inch natural straw hat with 2-inch-diameter opening
1-1/2-ounce nut cup (1-1/4 inches high x 2 inches across top)
Nuts or candies of choice

6-inch square of clear or colored plastic wrap
12-inch x 15-inch piece of white tulle netting
12 inches of 1/4-inch-wide satin picot ribbon—red or color of choice

Finished Size: Straw hat nut cup measures about 3-1/2 inches across x 4-1/2 inches long x 2 inches high.

Directions:
Fill nut cup with nuts or candies of choice. Cover nut cup with plastic wrap.

Insert covered nut cup into opening of hat.

Wrap hat in tulle netting, bringing the

ends together at narrow end of hat.

Tie ribbon in a bow around tulle close to brim of hat as shown in the photo above. Trim ribbon to desired length.

Cake's Topped off with Good Luck!

The uniquely country toppers crafted by Laura Goldman really take the wedding cake!

"Several brides-to-be have asked me to come up with custom cake toppers for them, so I've experimented with different looks," the cake decorator writes from Jefferson, Oregon.

"This double horseshoe design is a particular favorite of mine. It's easy to construct...plus, it brings good luck," she chuckles.

(Wondering about Laura's other designs? Send a self-addressed stamped envelope to her at P.O. Box 935, Jefferson OR 97352 for more details. Plan ahead, though—shipment for custom orders takes 4-6 weeks.)

Materials Needed:
Patterns below
Tracing paper and pencil
6-inch x 9-inch piece of corrugated cardboard or foam board
Purchased 4-7/8-inch-diameter x 1-3/4-inch-high white plastic cake topper base—available in bridal sections of most craft stores
28 inches of 2-1/4-inch-wide white beading lace
1/2 yard of 3/8-inch-wide natural jute braid
2-inch circle of 1-inch-thick white Styrofoam
2 yards of 7/8-inch-wide white taffeta craft ribbon or white grosgrain ribbon
1-1/4 yards of 1/2-inch-wide white braid trim
Nine 1/4-inch ribbon roses—teal or color of choice
Three 1-1/2-inch-long white organdy and silk rosebuds
Organdy flowers with 1-inch to 1-1/2-inch-wide blossoms—four white and five teal or similar flowers in colors of choice
Three 2-1/2-inch-long white silk fern fronds
Six white bridal picks with pearl accents
Low-temperature glue gun and glue sticks
Wire cutters
Scissors
Craft knife

Finished Size: Horseshoe cake topper is about 8 inches across x 7-1/2 inches high.

Directions:
Trace patterns below onto folded tracing paper. Cut out shapes and open for complete patterns. Trace around each pattern onto cardboard or foam board. Use the craft knife to cut out the horse-

HORSESHOE CAKE TOPPER PATTERNS
Trace 1 each—folded tracing paper
Cut 1 each—corrugated cardboard or foam board

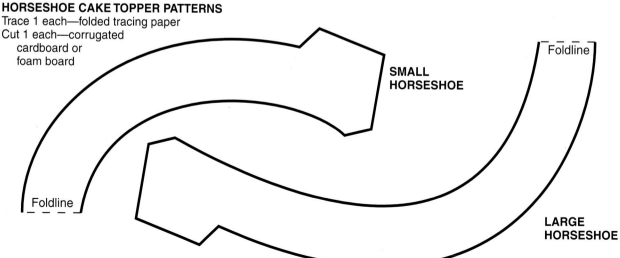

SMALL HORSESHOE

Foldline

LARGE HORSESHOE

Foldline

shoes on the traced lines.

Wrap each horseshoe with white taffeta or grosgrain ribbon, covering each completely and gluing ends of ribbon to secure. Trim excess ribbon.

Glue white braid to flat side of front and back of each horseshoe as shown in the photo at far left.

Referring to the photo for placement, glue the ribbon roses to the front of each horseshoe.

Thread natural jute braid through openings in beading lace. Then wrap lace around base of cake topper, gathering lace to fit base of topper. Overlap and glue ends in back. Trim excess. Distribute lace evenly around cake topper base. Spot-glue lace to cake topper as needed.

Glue Styrofoam circle to center top of cake topper.

Glue the back of the rounded portion of the small horseshoe to front edge of foam circle, tilting small horseshoe slightly to one side as shown in photo. Insert the large horseshoe into foam circle about 1 in. behind the small horseshoe, facing and tilting the large horseshoe in the same direction as shown in photo. Glue large horseshoe in place.

Glue white organdy and silk rosebuds to right front, center and left back of small horseshoe. Add remaining flowers, fern fronds and bridal picks around and between horseshoes as shown in the photo.

Simple Floral Straw Hats Head Bridal Decor Toward Country

Topping off Krista and Tony Reed's ranch wedding were homegrown touches like these flower-crowned cowboy hat table toppers.

"We wanted our wedding to reflect our rural lifestyle," comments Krista from the Ellensburg, Washington spread she and Tony call home. "Most of the decorating we did ourselves.

"My mom, Jeanne Kelly, came up with the idea of trimming straw hats for centerpieces at the reception. They were so popular, most were worn home by our guests!"

Materials Needed (for both):
Craft wire
Wire cutters
Low-temperature glue gun and glue sticks
Scissors

Materials Needed (for lady's hat):
Adult size natural straw cowboy hat
2 yards of 6-inch-wide white tulle netting
20 inches of green and white ivy garland
Three bearded wheat stems
Silk flowers—two white bridal sprays and one pink floral stem with several 1/2-inch blossoms or similar flowers in colors of choice

Materials Needed (for man's hat):
Adult size dark tan straw cowboy hat
Bandanna in color of choice
24 inches of green ivy garland
Two bearded wheat stems
Silk flowers—three teal floral stems with several 1/2-inch blossoms and several sprigs of small burgundy

flowers or similar flowers in colors of your choice

Finished Size: Each hat measures about 15 inches across.

Directions:
LADY'S HAT: Wrap tulle netting around hat where crown and brim meet. Tie ends of tulle netting in a bow at back of hat as shown in photo below. Spot-glue netting to hat to secure.

Cut ivy garland into two equal lengths. Tuck one end of each garland behind bow at back of hat. Bend garland around to front, following curve of hat. Spot-glue or wire garland to hat where crown and brim meet.

Trim stems from white bridal sprays and add one to each side of hat as shown in photo. Glue or wire to secure.

Glue or wire pink flowers to center of bow at back of hat. Add wheat stems where desired.

Trim the ends of the tulle netting to the length that looks best.

MAN'S HAT: Fold bandanna in half diagonally to make a triangle and then continue to fold bandanna, making a strip about 2 in. wide for hatband.

Wrap hatband around hat where crown and brim meet and tie ends in back of hat. Spot-glue to secure.

Glue or wire ivy garland around hat at base of hatband.

Trim ends of floral stems. Glue two teal floral stems to back of hat over tie of bandanna hatband and one to front of hat. Add burgundy flowers and wheat stems as desired.

Boot-Shaped Ring Pillow's Perfect For Walk Down a Country Aisle

With its lacy Victorian look, this fashionable lady's boot is sure to be "in step" at any country woman's wedding! Patsy Lowe of Abingdon, Virginia crafted the ring bearer's pillow for her daughter Valerie's nuptials.

"When we were visiting Western wear stores looking for wedding attire, a boot-shaped pillow caught Val's eye," Patsy penned.

"I decided to surprise her with a handmade version complete with ribbon and trims and a special cross-stitched message for her and Mike."

You can just as easily personalize the boot, too—just substitute the names of your bride and groom and their wedding date.

Materials Needed:

Patterns and chart on next page
Tracing paper and pencil
4-inch x 6-inch piece of 14-count white Aida cloth
DMC six-strand embroidery floss in colors listed on color key or in colors of choice
Size 24 tapestry needle
12-inch x 18-inch piece of white taffeta or fabric to match bride's dress
12-inch square of white lace or lace to match bride's dress
White all-purpose thread
Polyester stuffing
2 yards of 4mm white string pearls
6 yards of 1/8-inch-wide white satin ribbon
1/2 yard of 1/4-inch-wide white satin ribbon
Two silk burgundy open roses with 1-inch blossoms and leaves or similar flowers in color of choice
Standard sewing supplies
Low-temperature glue gun and glue sticks

Finished Size: Boot ring pillow measures about 10 inches high x 7 inches across. Design area of cross-stitched insert is 35 stitches high x 35 stitches wide.

Directions:

CROSS-STITCHING: Zigzag or overcast edges of Aida cloth to prevent fraying. Fold cloth in half, fold in half again to determine center and mark this point. To find center of chart, draw lines across chart connecting arrows. Begin stitching at this point so design will be centered.

Separate six-strand floss and use two strands for stitching design. Use one strand of pale mauve to stitch names and date. See Fig. 1 for stitch illustrations.

Each symbol on chart equals one stitch over a set of fabric threads with different symbols representing different colors or stitches. Make stitches in the colors shown on the chart or in your own colors, completing all cross-stitching first, then backstitching.

Do not knot the floss on back of the work. Instead, leave a short tail of floss and hold it in place while working the first few stitches around it. To end a strand, run needle under a few neighboring stitches in the back before cutting the floss close to work.

When all stitching is completed, and only if necessary, wash piece gently in lukewarm water and press right side down on terry towel to dry.

BOOT: Use copy machine to enlarge pattern to 200% or mark tracing paper with a 1-in. grid and draw pattern as shown onto tracing paper. Cut out boot shape from fabric as directed on pattern. Trim heel and toe portions from boot pattern, leaving lace overlay pattern. Cut lace overlay as directed on pattern.

Place lace overlay right sides up on right side of front and back of boot, matching top, bottom and side raw edges. Baste in place.

Cut out cross-stitched oval as indicated on boot pattern. Machine-stitch around edge with narrow zigzag. Pin completed cross-stitched oval right side up on top of lace overlay on front of boot as shown in photo. Machine-stitch close to edge to secure oval to boot.

Pin boot back and front right sides together with raw edges matching. Stitch around outside of boot with a 1/4-in. seam, leaving top open. Trim corners and clip curves.

Turn the boot right side out through opening. Stuff boot lightly. Turn raw edge of the opening in and hand-stitch the opening closed.

FINISHING: Glue pearl string to edge of cross-stitched oval and to heel and instep edges of lace overlay. Trim excess. Glue pearl string to outside edge of boot. Trim excess. Glue center of remaining pearl string to front of boot as shown in photo.

Cut a 5-1/2-in. length from 1/4-in.-wide ribbon for the hand loop on the back. Press ends 1/4 in. to wrong side. Center ribbon lengthwise on back of boot and hand-stitch ends to boot. Tie remaining 1/4-in.-wide ribbon in a bow to bottom of hand loop. Cut ends of ribbon at an angle to desired length.

Cut 1/8-in.-wide ribbon into six 36-in. lengths. Working with all six lengths as one, tie ribbon into a 5-in. multi-loop bow with long streamers as shown in Fig. 2. Glue bow to boot as shown in photo. Remove flowers from stems and glue flowers to center of bow.

Tie bride and groom's rings to streamers with an overhand knot. Tie overhand knots in ends of remaining streamers as shown in photo. Trim ends of streamers at an angle to desired lengths.

Fig. 1

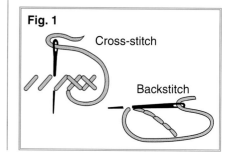

Cross-stitch

Backstitch

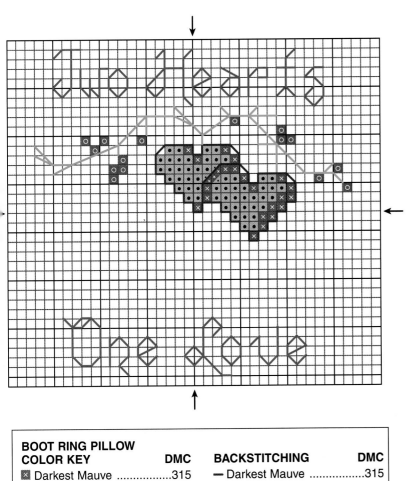

ALPHABET CHART AND NUMBERS
(for personalizing craft)

BOOT RING PILLOW

COLOR KEY	DMC	BACKSTITCHING	DMC
⊠ Darkest Mauve	315	— Darkest Mauve	315
◉ Dark Sage Green	500	— Dark Sage Green	500
• Pale Mauve	778	— Medium Sage Green	502

BOOT RING PILLOW PATTERNS

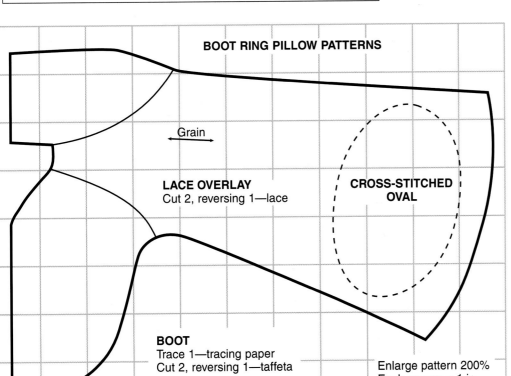

Grain

LACE OVERLAY
Cut 2, reversing 1—lace

CROSS-STITCHED OVAL

BOOT
Trace 1—tracing paper
Cut 2, reversing 1—taffeta

Enlarge pattern 200%
Each square = 1 in.

Fig. 2 Making multi-loop bow

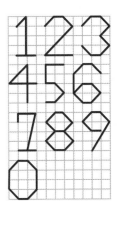

Heirloom Doily 'Cushions' Rings

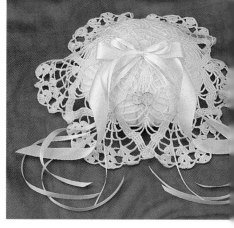

When Pat Harmon's two daughters got married in the same year, she had a *doubly* good reason to get crafting—they each planned to have a ring bearer in their ceremony.

"I designed a pillow that a youngster could easily carry without losing the rings, with a bow simple enough for the best man to untie," she describes from Depauw, Indiana.

"I used a family doily for each pillow...the result was a lovely keepsake."

Materials Needed:
14-inch round doily
Two 9-inch circles of satin to match doily
Matching all-purpose thread
Polyester stuffing
Matching satin ribbon—1 yard each of
*   1-inch-wide, 3/8-inch-wide and*
*   1/4-inch-wide, and 1-1/8 yards of*
*   1/8-inch-wide*
Two pearl bridal sprays (optional)

Standard sewing supplies

Finished Size: Doily ring pillow pictured measures about 14 inches across without ribbon streamers. Finished size will vary depending on size of doily used.

Directions:
Place 9-in. satin circles right sides together with edges matching. Stitch circles together with 1/2-in. seam, leaving opening for turning. Clip seam allowance. Turn pillow right side out through opening. Press.

Stuff pillow with polyester. Turn raw edges of opening in and hand-sew opening closed.

Center doily over one side of pillow. Hand-sew center to pillow. Smooth doily over pillow and lightly hand-tack doily to outside edge of pillow, hiding stitches in design of doily.

Hand-sew stems of pearl sprays to center of doily, making sure the pearls fan out from the center.

Tie the 1-in.-wide ribbon into a bow, leaving streamers about 12 in. long. Do the same with the 3/8-in.-wide ribbon and the 1/4-in.-wide ribbon.

Stack the ribbon bows with the widest ribbon on the bottom and the narrowest on the top. Hand-sew centers of stacked bows to pillow over pearl stems.

Hand-sew center of 1/8-in.-wide ribbon to pillow just below bows. Thread rings onto ribbon. Tie ends of ribbons together in a small bow to secure rings.

Basket Brims with Creative Trims

A tisket, a tasket, a "homegrown" flower girl basket! That's what little Karlee Whitcomb carried down the aisle at Stephanie and Robert Merritt's wedding in Bedford, Pennsylvania (see photo below far right).

Details Stephanie, "Robert's mother 'dressed up' a purchased white wicker basket with fringe, greens and tiny cowboy hats...then filled it with fresh rose petals for Karlee to scatter."

Materials Needed:
White wicker basket with 3-inch-high sides
3-1/2-inch-wide white fringe—length equal to measurement of outside top edge of basket
Dried materials—tree fern or other greenery and several sprigs of white baby's breath for top edge of basket
Four 2-inch-high silver plastic filigree hearts or other decorative hearts (available in bridal sections of most craft stores)
Two 2-inch white felt cowboy hats
Two white bridal sprays with pearl accents
1/2-inch-wide white satin or iridescent ribbon for wrapping handle of basket
Glue gun and glue sticks
Scissors
Fresh rose petals in color of choice

Finished Size: Basket pictured is about 9 inches across x 9 inches high, including handle. Finished size will vary depending on size of basket used.

Directions:
Wrap ribbon around handle of basket. Glue ends to inside of basket to secure. Trim excess ribbon.

Glue top of fringe to outside edge of basket as in photo at far left. Overlap and glue ends. Trim excess fringe.

Glue greenery and baby's breath to top edge of basket as shown in photo.

Glue two silver hearts to handle of one side of basket, overlapping them. Glue a cowboy hat to front of hearts and a bridal spray to handle above hearts. Repeat on other side of basket.

Fill basket with rose petals.

Paul Price

Pretty Fringed Pillow Is Soft on Romance!

Louise Ducharme of Wynndel, British Columbia added a charmingly romantic element to her wedding—with a heart-shaped ring bearer's pillow she fashioned herself.

You can easily do the same...just follow her heartfelt instructions below, using colors that fit your bridal theme.

Materials Needed:

Pattern below right
Tracing paper and pencil
Two 12-inch squares of white taffeta or fabric to match bride's dress
Two 12-inch squares of quilt batting
Polyester stuffing
1 yard of 3-inch-wide white fringe
1/8-inch-wide satin ribbon—20 inches each of purple and teal or colors of choice
1/2-inch ribbon roses—two purple and three teal or colors of choice
Three white silk roses with 1-inch blossoms
Spray of pearls on stem (found in bridal sections of most craft stores)
4 inches of 1/2-inch-wide white elastic
White all-purpose thread
Standard sewing supplies
Low-temperature glue gun and glue sticks

Finished Size: Heart ring pillow measures about 10 inches across x 9 inches high without fringe.

Directions:

Use copy machine to enlarge pattern to 200%, or mark tracing paper with a 1-in. grid and draw pattern as shown onto tracing paper.

Trace enlarged pattern onto folded tracing paper. Cut out and open for a complete pattern. Cut out heart from taffeta and quilt batting as directed on pattern.

Pin fabric hearts with right sides together and edges matching. Sew hearts together with a 1/4-in. seam, leaving opening between dots for turning as indicated on pattern. Trim point and clip curves. Turn the heart right side out through the opening.

Trim 1/4 in. from outside edge of each quilt batting heart. Place the two trimmed quilt batting heart shapes inside ring pillow and align the shapes, matching the outside edges of the quilt batting hearts with the stitched seam of the ring pillow.

Insert polyester stuffing between layers of batting to give the pillow a smooth look. Stuff firmly but do not overstuff so as not to distort heart shape. Turn raw edges of opening in. Hand-stitch opening closed.

Glue fringe to seam on outside edge of the ring pillow as shown in the photo below left.

Glue or hand-stitch pearl spray and white flowers at an angle to front of ring pillow as shown in photo. Place ribbon roses where desired and glue or hand-stitch them in place.

Cut a 6-in. piece of each color ribbon. Fold each ribbon in half to form a loop. Glue or hand-stitch ends of each loop to ring pillow so loops are visible and ends are hidden under flowers.

Fold each remaining length of ribbon in half. Apply a dot of glue to fold of each. Glue fold of each under flowers. Or hand-stitch folds to ring pillow. Tie bride's and groom's rings to these ribbons.

Center elastic across back of ring pillow and hand-stitch ends to ring pillow for hand loop.

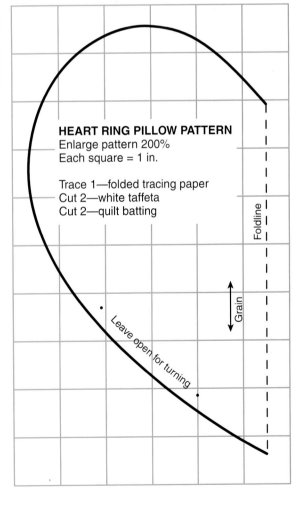

HEART RING PILLOW PATTERN
Enlarge pattern 200%
Each square = 1 in.

Trace 1—folded tracing paper
Cut 2—white taffeta
Cut 2—quilt batting

Foldline

Grain

Leave open for turning

Crocheted Topper Rings in Couples' Nuptials

Ask Lorraine Andrews of Houston, British Columbia to put some pretty accents on a wedding cake…and you'll soon find she's in stitches! She makes the rounds, designing cake toppers with popular bridal motifs such as these delicate crocheted bells.

Seasoned crocheters are sure to get "hooked" on her sound instructions below for stitching the bell topper.

A packet of six additional crocheted wedding cake topper patterns from Lorraine is available for $15 (U.S.). Write to her at P.O. Box 533, Houston BC Canada V0J 1Z0.

Materials Needed:
One ball of size 10 white crochet cotton
Size 6 (1.75mm) steel crochet hook
Stitch marker
Commercial fabric stiffener
6-inch x 22-inch piece of white tulle netting
White all-purpose thread and hand-sewing needle
Four white bridal picks with pearl accents
Pearl beads—twenty-three 4mm and twenty-two 8mm
14 inches of 20-gauge craft wire
Wire cutters
Aluminum foil
Plastic container with 3-inch-diameter bottom
Glue gun and glue sticks

Finished Size: Cake topper is about 8 inches tall x 7 inches across.

Special Abbreviations:
SHELL: SH(S): Work (3 tr, ch 3, 3 tr) in sp indicated.
SHELL IN SHELL: SH in SH: Work a SH in ch-sp of SH of previous round.

Directions:
BELLS (make three): Round 1: Ch 5, join with sl st in first ch to form a ring.

Round 2: Ch 1 (counts as sc), work 9 scs into ring, join with sl st in beginning ch-1: 10 scs.

Round 3: Ch 3 (counts as dc), work 1 dc in sl st, work 2 dc in each of the next scs around, join with sl st in beginning ch-3: 20 dcs.

Round 4: Ch 4 and work (2 tr, ch 3, 3 tr) in sl st (counts as first SH here and throughout), sk 1 dc, work 1 tr in next dc; * sk 1 dc, SH in next dc, sk 1 dc, work 1 tr in next dc; repeat from * around, join with sl st in top of beginning ch-4: 5 SHS.

Round 5: Sl st to ch-3 sp, ch 4 and work (2 tr, ch 3, 3 tr) in same ch-3 sp, work 1 tr in tr between SHS of previous round; * SH in SH, work 1 tr in tr between SHS of previous round; repeat from * around, join with sl st in top of beginning ch-4: 5 SHS.

Round 6: Sl st to ch-3 sp, ch 4 and work (2 tr, ch 3, 3 tr) in same ch-3 sp, ch 1, work 1 tr in tr between SHS of previous round, ch 1; * SH in SH, ch 1, work 1 tr in tr between SHS of previous round, ch 1; repeat from * around, join with sl st in top of beginning ch-4: 5 SHS.

Round 7: Sl st to ch-3 sp, ch 4 and work (2 tr, ch 3, 3 tr) in same ch-3 sp, ch 2, work 1 tr in tr between SHS of previous round, ch 2; * SH in SH, ch 2, work 1 tr in next tr, ch 2; repeat from * around, join with sl st in top of beginning ch-4: 5 SHS.

Round 8: Sl st to ch-3 sp, ch 4 and work (2 tr, ch 3, 3 tr) in same ch-3 sp, ch 2, work (1 tr, ch 3, 1 tr) in tr between SHS of previous round, ch 2; * SH in SH, ch 2, work (1 tr, ch 3, 1 tr) in next tr between SHS of previous round, ch 2; repeat from * around, join with sl st in top of beginning ch-4: 5 SHS.

Round 9: Sl st to ch-3 sp, ch 4 and work (2 tr, ch 3, 3 tr) in same ch-3 sp, ch 2, work (1 tr, ch 3, 1 tr) in next ch-3 sp, ch 2; * SH in SH, ch 2, work (1 tr, ch 3, 1 tr) in next ch-3 sp, ch 2; repeat from * around, join with sl st in top of beginning ch-4: 5 SHS.

Round 10: Sl st to ch-3 sp, ch 4 and work (2 tr, ch 3, 3 tr) in same sp, ch 2, work (1 tr, ch 2, 1 tr, ch 2, 1 tr) in next ch-3 sp, ch 2; * SH in SH, ch 2, work (1 tr, ch 2, 1 tr, ch 2, 1 tr) in next ch-3 sp, ch 2; repeat from * around, join with sl st to beginning ch-4.

Round 11: * Ch 6, sc in ch-3 sp of SH, ch 6, sc in last tr of SH, ch 6, sk next ch-2 sp, [sc in next ch-2 sp, ch 6] twice, sk next ch-2 sp, sc in first tr of next SH; repeat from * around, join with sl st in first ch of ch-6. Fasten off and weave in loose ends.

STAND: Round 1: Ch 5, join with sl st in first ch to form a ring.

Round 2: Ch 2 (counts as sc), work 10 scs into ring, join with sl st in top of beginning ch-2: 11 scs.

Round 3: Ch 3 (counts as dc here and throughout), work 1 dc in sl st, work 2 dcs in each dc around, join with sl st in top of beginning ch-3: 22 dcs.

Round 4: Ch 3, work 1 dc in sl st, dc in next dc; * work 2 dcs in next dc, dc in next dc; repeat from * around, join with sl st in top of beginning ch-3: 33 dcs.

Round 5: Ch 3, work 1 dc in sl st, dc in each of next two dcs; * work 2 dcs in next dc, dc in each of next two dcs; repeat from * around, join with sl st in top of beginning ch-3: 44 dcs.

Round 6: Ch 3, work 1 dc in sl st, dc in each of next three dcs; * work 2 dcs in next dc, dc in each of next three dcs; repeat from * around, join with sl st in top

ABBREVIATIONS

ch(s)   chain(s)
dc(s)   double crochet(s)
hk   hook
lp(s)   loop(s)
sc(s)   single crochet(s)
sk   skip or skipped
sl st   slip stitch
sp   space
st(s)   stitch(es)
tr(s)   treble crochet(s)
yo   yarn over
* () or [] Instructions following asterisk or between parentheses or brackets are repeated as indicated.

of beginning ch-3: 55 dcs.

Round 7: Ch 3, work 1 dc in sl st, dc in each of next four dcs; * work 2 dcs in next dc, dc in each of next four dcs; repeat from * around, join with sl st in top of beginning ch-3: 66 dcs.

Round 8: Ch 3, work 1 dc in sl st, dc in each of next five dcs; * work 2 dcs in next dc, dc in each of next five dcs; repeat from * around, join with sl st in top of beginning ch-3: 77 dcs.

Round 9: Ch 3, work 1 dc in sl st, dc in each of next six dcs; * work 2 dcs in next dc, dc in each of next six dcs; repeat from * around, join with sl st in top of beginning ch-3; place stitch marker at end of round: 88 dcs.

Round 10: Ch 3, work 1 dc in each dc around, join with sl st in top of beginning ch-3.

Round 11: Ch 1; * sk next 3 dc, work (4 tr, ch 3, 4 tr) in next dc, sk next 3 dc, sc in next dc; repeat from * around, join with sl st to beginning ch-1: 11 tr groups.

Round 12: Sl st to center ch of ch-3 sp, ch 4, work 6 tr in same center ch, ch 3; * work 7 tr in center ch of next ch-3 sp, ch 3; repeat from * around, join with sl st in top of beginning ch-4: 11 sets of 7 trs.

Round 13: Sl st to fourth tr; * ch 7, sc in ch-3 sp, ch 7, sc in fourth tr; repeat from * around, ch 7, join with sl st to be-ginning ch of ch-7: 22 ch-7 sps.

Round 14: Sl st to fourth ch of ch-7 sp; * ch 8, sc in fourth ch of ch-7; repeat from * around, join with sl st to first ch of beginning ch-8. Fasten off.

TOP EDGING OF STAND: Round 1: With right side facing, fold stand between Rows 9 and 10 with wrong sides together. Insert hk at marker at end of Round 9 and join with sl st, ch 2, sc between each dc around, join with sl st in top of beginning ch-2: 88 scs.

Round 2: * Ch 7, sk 3 sc, sc in next sc; repeat from * around, join with sl st to first ch of beginning ch-7: 22 ch-7 sps.

Round 3: Sl st to fourth ch of ch-7; * ch 7, sc in next ch-7 sp; repeat from * around, join with sl st to first ch of beginning ch-7. Fasten off.

STIFFENING: Apply stiffener to stand, following manufacturer's instructions. Dry stand right side out over inverted plastic container, shaping Round 11 so it will stand as shown in photo.

Crumple and shape aluminum into three bell shapes the size of the crocheted bells. Apply stiffener to bells as before. Place bells right side out over aluminum forms. Let dry, shaping them as needed to maintain bell shape as shown in photo.

PEARL HEART: Thread pearl beads onto craft wire, alternating large and small pearls. Twist ends of wire together to hold.

With twist of wire at bottom point of heart, form pearl-covered wire into heart shape as shown in photo.

FINISHING: Cut an 18-in.-long piece from tulle netting. Fold strip in half lengthwise. Thread needle with white thread and hand-sew along long edge 1/4 in. from fold to gather edge. Draw up thread to form tulle into a circle. Fasten off thread. Glue tulle circle to center top of base of cake topper. Let dry.

Cut remaining tulle netting into two 2-in. x 6-in. pieces. Hand-sew 1/4 in. from one long edge of both pieces, leaving thread attached to gather both pieces as one. Draw up thread to form tulle into a circle. Fasten off thread. Insert twisted wire of beaded heart into center of tulle circle. Glue to hold.

Glue bottom edges of bells to top edge of cake topper stand as shown in photo. Glue tops of bells together where they meet.

Glue a bridal pick inside each bell.

Cut flowers from remaining bridal pick. Glue a single flower to center of tulle circle on base of cake topper. Glue another flower to point of beaded heart. Glue rest of bridal pick to top of heart as shown in the photo. Glue beaded heart to top of bells.

Inspirations for Invitations

STUFFY FORMAL invitations just don't seem to set the right tone for folks planning weddings that include horses, wagons, Western attire, wildflowers and picnic suppers.

The following couples crafted their own invites to let guests know that their special day would be a unique celebration with a fun, relaxed, down-home country atmosphere.

♥ When cowboy Shane Randall of Ririe, Idaho and his fiancee, Judy Moore, decided to get hitched, they planned a simple outdoor wedding. They chose single-sheet 8- x 10-inch invitations showing a misty scene of a cowboy herding horses, along with cowboy lingo to announce the event.

♥ To round up guests for her wedding to John, Lizz Gelwicks of Stillman Valley, Illinois custom-designed their invitations. She explains, "On the cover was a picture of a barn and the saying, 'Through wooin' and courtin' our dreams have been spun, and our lifetime together has just begun!' "

♥ When Greg and Rebekah Earle were married country-style in Westlock, Alberta, they farmed out the job of creating invitations to his mom, Ruth Earle. She embossed the cover in gold with stalks of barley tied with a bow. Inside, she carried over the theme by attaching a small raffia bow.

♥ Leslie and Bill Greene exchanged vows wearing ice skates on a frozen pond east of Peterborough, Ontario beneath a birch-bark arch. They used the same natural look for their invitations, copying a verse onto paper and gluing it to birch-bark cards. At the reception, their three single-layer cakes were set on short birch-bark stumps.

♥ "WANTED: Friends and family who are not afraid of having a good time at a wedding," began the clever "wanted poster" tucked into the invitations of Jim and Deb Henderson of Maroa, Illinois. The handy note also let guests know Western dress was appropriate. It ended: "Come prepared to dance the night away and have a rootin'-tootin' good time!"

An Old-West Motif Colors Couple's Decor

For their "getting hitched" ceremony, Becky and Mike Bell got on a roll with an Old-West theme, jots mother-of-the-bride Cheryl Klotz from Bonney Lake, Washington.

"The whole family helped with the decorations," she informs. "We turned the serving tables into covered wagons and used one for the gift table as well. The guests' tables were covered with red-and-white checked tablecloths.

"Table toppers designed by Becky's Aunt Jerri included small covered wagons made from Popsicle sticks with red bandanna material for the tops.

"Her great-aunts came up with the idea of dressing up baskets with bandanna skirts and raffia bows. They were perfect for holding silverware, wedding cards on the gift table, etc."

Materials Needed (for one wagon):
26 craft or Popsicle sticks
Two craft picks or round toothpicks
Sharp craft scissors or scroll saw
Four 1-1/2-inch-diameter plastic game pieces or poker chips for wheels
4-1/2-inch x 8-inch piece of print fabric or bandanna fabric—red or color of choice
Matching all-purpose thread
Two 8-inch pieces of 16-gauge craft wire
Waxed paper or plastic wrap
Glue gun and glue sticks
Standard sewing supplies

Finished Size: Covered wagon is about 6 inches long x 2-3/4 inches wide x 5-1/2 inches high.

Directions:
Cover flat work surface with waxed paper or plastic wrap. Work on covered surface when gluing craft sticks together.

Place two craft sticks 3 in. apart on covered surface for uprights of one side of wagon. Glue three craft sticks to uprights, leaving 1/2 in. between each as shown in Fig. 1. Repeat for the other side of the wagon.

Glue edges of six craft sticks together with ends even to form bottom of wagon. Then glue a craft stick diagonally across them as shown in Fig. 2 to brace the bottom.

Using craft scissors or scroll saw, cut eight craft sticks in half crosswise.

Glue edges of five half-craft sticks together with cut edges even as shown in Fig. 3 for front panel of wagon. Repeat, using five more half-craft sticks for back panel of wagon.

Cut a length from craft stick equal to the width of the front panel. Glue craft stick to front panel 3/8 in. from top edge for brace as shown in Fig. 3.

Repeat, using remainder of the craft stick for the back of the wagon.

Glue a half-craft stick centered lengthwise to edge of each side of front and back panels for side rails as shown in Fig. 3.

Glue long edges of wagon bottom to bottom edge of each side, making sure ends are even.

Glue front panel to bottom and sides of wagon with side rails of front panel aligned with uprights of each wagon side. Glue back panel to back of wagon in same way.

Cut two 2-in.-long pieces from craft picks or toothpicks. Glue one end of each to each end of brace of front panel. Glue other ends together for hitch as shown in photo at far left below.

Glue long edges of two half-craft sticks together to make L-shaped seat as shown in Fig. 4. Glue seat to front of wagon above hitch as shown in photo.

Glue a plastic game piece or poker chip to the bottom end of each upright for wheels as shown in photo.

Press 1/4 in. to wrong side on each short edge of red print fabric for side edges of wagon cover.

For front and back of wagon cover, turn 1/4 in. to wrong side on each long edge of fabric. Stitch a scant 1/4 in. from each fold to make a channel.

Thread a piece of craft wire through each channel, gathering fabric as needed to fit. Bend 1/4 in. of each end of wires to inside to hold fabric in place.

Center and glue one pressed edge of fabric cover (edge without the wire insert) along top craft stick on outside of one side of wagon box. Bend craft wires over top of wagon to other side of wagon, making an inverted U and covering uprights as shown in photo.

Glue other pressed edge of fabric centered along top craft stick on outside of other side of wagon box. Shape

Fig. 1 Making wagon sides

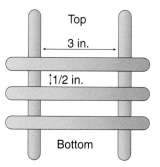

Fig. 2 Making wagon bottom

Top

3 in.

1/2 in.

Bottom

Fig. 3 Making wagon ends

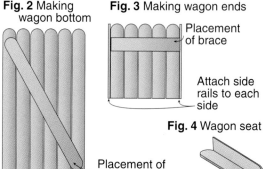

Placement of brace

Attach side rails to each side

Fig. 4 Wagon seat

Placement of diagonal craft stick

the craft wire and distribute the fabric along the wire to form wagon top as shown in the photo.

Materials Needed (for one basket):
Market basket with handle
Red print fabric or bandanna fabric or print fabric in color of choice—amount equal to twice the distance around the rim of your basket x the height of your basket plus 3-1/4 inches
1-1/2-inch-wide pre-gathered white lace—amount equal to distance around the rim of your basket plus twice the length of the handle
Matching all-purpose thread
Standard sewing supplies
Silk flowers—two miniature white daises and four miniature sunflowers
Several strands of natural raffia
Craft wire
Glue gun and glue sticks
Craft scissors

Finished Size: Card basket pictured is 18 inches long x 10 inches wide x 12 inches high. Size of card basket will vary depending on size of market basket.

Directions:
Trim a 2-in.-wide strip from long edge of fabric for basket and set remaining fabric aside. Wrap handle of basket with strip, covering completely. Trim excess and glue end to handles to secure.

Sew short ends of remaining fabric piece with right sides together and 1/4-in. seams, making a large tube of fabric.

Fold and press one long edge 3/4 in. to wrong side. Stitch a row of gathering stitches 1/4 in. from fold. Stitch another row of gathering stitches 1/2 in. from fold. Draw up both rows of gathering stitches to fit outside rim of basket.

Place covering right side out over top rim of basket, distributing fullness evenly around basket. Fasten off gathering threads. Spot-glue gathered edge to the rim of the basket to secure.

Glue gathered edge of lace to top rim of basket as shown in photo above. Glue two pieces of lace to handle of basket, leaving a band of fabric exposed.

Cut several 7-in.-long pieces of raffia. Stack raffia into a small bundle. Wrap center of bundle with craft wire to secure. Glue bundle of raffia to outside of basket handle as shown in photo. Make and attach another bundle of raffia to other side of basket.

Cut two 2-in. x 12-in. strips of fabric. Tie each strip into a small bow. Glue a bow to center of each raffia bundle.

Glue two sunflowers and a daisy to each side of handle above bows.

Tuck raw edges of fabric cover under the basket.

Tables Brim with Sunflower Trims

A sunny day was definitely in the forecast for Dianne and Paul Handsaker's outdoor Western wedding in Apple Canyon Lake, Illinois.

"For decorations, we filled antique milk cans with sunflowers, red carnations, button mums and daisies, then tied bows of raffia to the handles," Dianne describes.

"At the reception, mason jars holding sunflowers were trimmed with raffia and ribbon and served as table toppers. A votive candle glowed from the top of each one."

Materials Needed (for one candle holder):
Quart-size canning jar with regular-size opening
2-5/8-inch-wide x 2-1/2-inch-high clear glass flowerpot or candle holder (must be slightly bigger than opening of canning jar so it will sit on top, not slip down)
Votive or tea candle
Several silk flowers—sunflowers with 3-inch blossoms or similar flowers in colors of choice (Dianne also used daisies in some of her jars)
6 inches of silk ivy garland or other greens
Several strands of natural raffia
1/8-inch-wide satin ribbon —1 yard each of green and yellow or two different colors of choice
Craft scissors

Finished Size: Candle holder is about 8 inches high x 4 inches across.

Directions:
Trim stems of sunflowers so flowers will fit inside canning jar. Arrange sunflowers and the ivy garland as desired inside the jar, making sure that flowers face in all directions.

Cut raffia into 1-yd. lengths. Wrap green and yellow ribbon and several strands of raffia as one around top of jar. Tie ends in a bow as shown in the photo to far left.

Place votive or tea candle inside glass flowerpot or candle holder. Set in rim of canning jar.

If desired, place several sunflowers on either side of jar to complete table arrangement.

Cards Can Easily Be Tucked into Chuck Wagon

A wagonload of fun was had by everyone attending Naomi and Philip Schellenberg's Western-flavored wedding reception (see photo at right), confirms the bride's mom, Rhonda Berstad of Melfort, Saskatchewan.

"We decorated with rural accents like hay bales, saddles, cowboy hats, boots and bridles," she notes.

"Naomi's grandmother came up with the idea of crafting and painting a chuck wagon to hold all of the wedding cards."

Materials Needed:

Pattern on next page
Tracing paper and pencil
66 inches of 4-inch-wide x 1/4-inch-thick basswood
One 14-inch-long piece of 1-inch-wide x 1/2-inch-thick pine
Two 5-inch-long pieces of 1-inch dowel for axles of wagon
Scroll saw
Drill with 1/8-inch bit
Sandpaper and tack cloth
Four 1-inch wood screws and screwdriver
Three wire coat hangers for wire hoops of wagon top
Wire cutters
18-1/2-inch square of 100% cotton unbleached muslin or homespun fabric for wagon top
Matching all-purpose thread
1-1/3 yards of off-white lightweight cord or pearl cotton
Tapestry needle
Acrylic craft paint—dark green or color of choice
Small flat paintbrush
2-1/2-inch x 3-inch piece of lightweight cardboard
Black permanent marker
Glue gun and glue sticks
Standard sewing supplies

Finished Size: Covered wagon card holder is about 13 inches high x 14 inches long x 6 inches wide.

Directions:

Trace wheel pattern onto folded tracing paper. Cut out as directed and open for a complete pattern.

Trace around pattern four times onto 1/4-in.-thick basswood.

Use scroll saw to cut out four wheels.

From basswood, use scroll saw to cut two 4-in. x 12-in. pieces for sides, one 4-in. x 11-1/2-in. piece for bottom and two 4-in. squares for ends of wagon.

From 14-in.-long piece of pine, cut a 1/4-in.-thick x 1/2-in.-wide strip for center brace of wagon top. Cut remaining 14-in.-long piece of pine into six 2-in.-long pieces for wire hoop holders.

Drill a hole through the center of each wheel where indicated on the pattern and into the center of one end of each wire hoop holder. Also drill a pilot hole in the center of each end of each axle.

Sand all wood pieces until smooth and wipe with tack cloth.

Paint all surfaces of wood pieces dark green or desired color. Let dry.

Referring to Assembly Diagram, glue sides to bottom of wagon and then glue front and back ends in place to make wagon box. Prop pieces to hold them in place until glue sets.

Glue a 2-in.-long wooden wire hoop holder (drilled hole up) to each end of one side of wagon box. Glue another wire hoop holder centered along inside of same side of wagon. Glue remaining wire hoop holders to inside of other

ASSEMBLY DIAGRAM

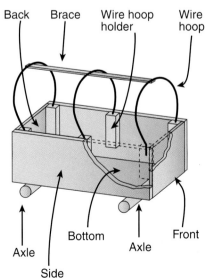

side of wagon box in the same way.

Cut a 20-in.-long piece of wire from each wire coat hanger. Gently bend wires into an inverted U-shape for hoops of wagon.

Insert each end of one wire hoop into drilled holes of wire hoop holders on opposite sides of wagon. Add glue as needed to secure hoops. Repeat with two remaining wire hoops.

Position 14-in.-long brace across top of wire hoops. Glue brace to hoops so ends of brace are even with front and back wire hoops. See Assembly Diagram.

Glue axles to bottom of wagon box where shown in Assembly Diagram. Use wood screws to attach a wheel to each end of axles.

Press 1/4 in. along one side of muslin or homespun fabric for wagon top to wrong side. Fold 1/4 in. again to wrong side and stitch close to edge of first fold to hem. Repeat on opposite edge.

Press 1/4 in. to wrong side along the remaining edges of the wagon top. Fold each 1/4 in. again to wrong side and stitch close to edges of the first fold to

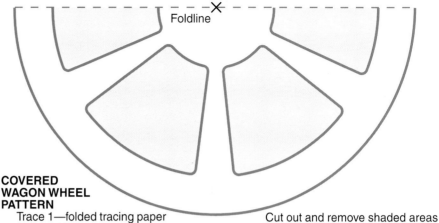

COVERED WAGON WHEEL PATTERN
Trace 1—folded tracing paper
Cut 4—1/4-in. basswood

Cut out and remove shaded areas
X = drilled hole

make a channel.

Thread tapestry needle with cord or pearl cotton. Insert a 24-in. length of cord or pearl cotton into each channel.

Place wagon top right side out over wire hoops with stitched channels at the front and back of wagon. Glue or staple a hemmed edge of wagon top to outside of each side of wagon, making sure top

is centered over the hoops and along the length of the wagon.

Draw up cord or pearl cotton and tie into a bow at each end of wagon.

Use the black permanent marker to write "JUST MARRIED" on the piece of lightweight cardboard. Glue the sign to end of covered wagon as shown in photo at far left.

Horseshoe Holder's a Real Ringer

Horseplay was definitely okay the day Cynthia Malchow and Gary Wiggins tied the knot at the Malchow ranch in Castle Rock, Colorado!

"Both of them love horses and ranching, so it was only fitting that the event had a Western theme," explains mother-of-the-bride Jeanette.

"Even the ring holder was rustic. We embellished a horseshoe with silk flowers and a miniature straw bale, then tucked the wedding band on top."

Materials Needed:
Horseshoe (any size)
Mini straw bale in size appropriate for size of horseshoe
Silk flowers—two picks with several 1/2-inch pink blossoms and two picks with several tiny blue blossoms or similar flowers in colors of choice
Wire cutters
Glue gun and glue sticks
Floral adhesive or greening pin to hold ring
Groom's ring

Finished Size: Horseshoe ring holder measures about 5-1/2 inches across x 5 inches high.

Directions:
Cut flowers from picks, leaving stems 2

to 3 in. long.

Glue flowers to horseshoe with stems pointing toward curve of horseshoe.

Glue the mini straw bale centered over the stems of the flowers as shown in the photo above.

Make a depression in top of mini straw bale for ring. Place a bit of floral adhesive inside depression and insert ring into depression. Or place ring into depression and use greening pin to hold ring in place.

Feed Sacks Stack Up as Fun Favors

Rather than having guests toss rice or birdseed after she and her groom, Gene, exchanged wedding vows, Kimberly Mumaw of Wooster, Ohio (below right) picked a rustic alternative.

"We chose wheat seed instead because it symbolizes prosperity and good fortune," she relates. "I tied up small piles in squares of fabric to create little 'feed bags'.

"As folks signed the guest book, they each received one. Everyone got a kick out of them," Kimberly confirms. "Plus, the leftovers made nice mementos."

Materials Needed (for each):
6-1/2-inch square of chambray or
*   bandanna fabric or other fabric in*
*   color of choice*
12 inches of 3-ply natural jute string
2 tablespoons of wheat seed
Pinking shears

Finished Size: Each wheat sack favor is about 3-1/2 inches high x 1-1/2 inches across.

Directions:
Trim each edge of fabric square with pinking shears, making a 6-in. square of fabric.

Place fabric wrong side up on a flat surface. Spoon wheat seed onto center of square.

Bring opposite corners of fabric together. Repeat, tucking sides of fabric in so wheat does not fall out.

Wrap jute string tightly around fabric just above wheat, making a small sack as shown in photo below left. Tie ends of jute string into a small bow. Trim ends of jute to desired length.

From Head to Toe, Hall's Decked Out in Country

Amy Riesberg (far right above) of Carroll, Iowa found a unique way to outline the Western theme she and her husband, Jay, chose for their rural union—with these fitting silhouettes.

"We cut out the cowboy hat and boots from tagboard and colored paper and used them to decorate the walls at our reception hall," she comments. "They looked pretty and cost next to nothing."

You can quickly do the same, thanks to the easy instructions Amy shares here. Or come up with motifs of your own, such as horseshoes, a cactus, a prancing pony—or anything you like!

Materials Needed (for both):
Patterns on next page
Tracing paper and pencil
12-inch x 18-inch piece of tagboard
*   or poster board*
12-inch x 18-inch piece of mylar or

metallic tissue paper—red and
black or colors of choice
Spray adhesive
Scissors
Removable poster tape or
double-stick tape

Finished Size: Boot measures 9 inches across x 10-1/2 inches high. Hat measures 13-1/2 inches across x 8-1/4 inches high.

Directions:
Use copy machine to enlarge boot and hat patterns to 200% and cut out. Or mark tracing paper with a 1-in. grid and draw patterns as shown onto tracing paper and cut out.

Trace around each pattern onto back side of tagboard or poster board.

Spray front side of board with spray adhesive. Place mylar or metallic tissue paper over sprayed board and smooth out wrinkles.

Cut out shapes, following traced lines on back.

Use removable poster tape or double-stick tape on back for mounting.

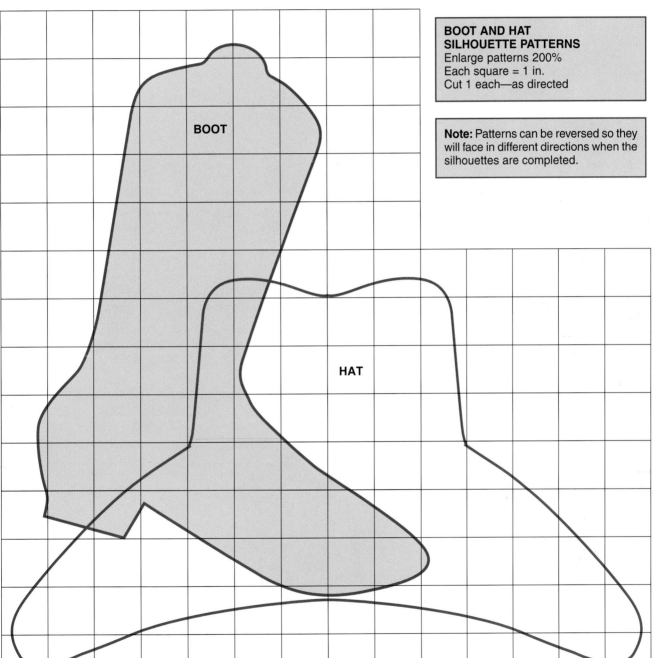

BOOT

HAT

**BOOT AND HAT
SILHOUETTE PATTERNS**
Enlarge patterns 200%
Each square = 1 in.
Cut 1 each—as directed

Note: Patterns can be reversed so they will face in different directions when the silhouettes are completed.

Love Takes Them for a Ride

A little horsing around was in order when Gina Gerberding and Bill Hudson decided to get hitched in Belvidere, Nebraska!

SADDLE PALS Gina and Bill Hudson let love have free rein in Belvidere, Nebraska. "We used a ladder to get Gina aboard in her dress," Mom Marla Gerberding pens.

Photos: Creekside Photography, Blue Hill, Neb.

BEAUTIFUL DREAMER, Gina first envisioned her country wedding as a young girl. Romantic musings materialized in flowers, bridesmaids dresses and a wedding hat, which she designed.

BRIDAL SWEET. Gina's cake called for a pinch of flowers. Rosebuds and foliage were the icing on the cake. A golden cowboy boot vase was in step with her theme.

DRAWING STRAWS into bale benches accommodated a bumper crop of guests. The groom's parents' yard was decked with a white arbor and garden flowers.

A SHOE-IN idea Bill and Gina had for table centerpieces was this horseshoe candle holder. Well-worn ringers came from the newlyweds' sure-footed steeds!

UNDER THEIR HATS, Bill and groomsmen have a strong sense of cowboy style. Bill proposed between team penning events in which he and Gina were partners. They now raise quarter horses.

This Bride Glides into Married Life

AMID a winter wonderland, Leslie Hunter and Bill Greene laced up their skates and tied the knot on an ice-covered pond east of Peterborough, Ontario.

"Our entire wedding party was on skates…including the minister," Leslie says of the heartwarming nuptials held at The Hunter Farm Bed-and-Breakfast owned by her parents. "Suits and ties weren't recommended for guests—but boots and parkas were.

"My father drove me to the site in a one-horse sleigh I'd refurbished for the occasion," Leslie remembers.

"In place of a procession, the wedding party skated around the pond as our guests looked on from wooden plank and hay bale benches. We were married on the pond in front of a birch bark archway my father built from logs cut from our property."

Leslie designed the wedding invitations and floral arrangements, plus her bridal gown and bridesmaids dresses. To reflect the dazzling hues of winter, she chose ice blue, snow white and shimmering silver colors.

"My bridesmaids and I wore silk crepe dresses, velvet capes and fur-trimmed headbands and muffs," she describes their chic yet snugly attire. "The groomsmen were comfortable in matching fleece sweaters. And Bill wore a Nordic-style pullover hand-knit by one of our friends."

After exchanging vows, the bride and groom joined their guests for a February afternoon packed with "wintertainment".

"We enjoyed sleigh rides, hockey, tobogganing and cross-country skiing," Leslie reports. "At sunset, we gathered at the farmhouse for a country buffet of lasagna, chicken potpie, rice and salads.

"The flower baskets on the tables were accented with brilliant red dogwood twigs. We fashioned birch stumps into natural pedestals for the three cakes that were topped with shaved white chocolate to resemble snowflakes.

"The beauty of winter was so much a part of our wedding," Leslie confirms. "I even carried it into the thank-you note message I composed as a variation of *Jingle Bells*."

As Leslie likes to tell it, a dash of snow and a jingle of sweet wintry memories will be making Bill's and her spirits bright for a lifetime!

Editor's Note: *Leslie Greene has her own home business, Leslie Marie Bridal Designs. To contact her, call 1-416/236-7255. You can reach The Hunter Farm B&B at 1-705/295-6253.*

COLD FEET were expected when Leslie Hunter and Bill Greene (above) tied the knot on an iced-over pond! Guests watched from the shore as a warmly dressed bridal party skated out for "I do's".

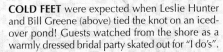

101

Their Nuptials Show How the West Was Fun

Old-West elements added charm to Becky Klotz and Mike Bell's wedding celebration in the historic town of Buckley, Washington.

HEAD-TURNING bride Becky Bell and her attendants rounded up for a nostalgic photo in front of an antique wheel on the historical society grounds near Buckley, Washington. "The flower girl and ring bearer trotted in on stick horses," shares the bride's mom, Cheryl Klotz.

OVERARCHING HUMOR was in play at Mike and Becky's hitchin' post. "Our family's full of practical jokers," she notes of the rope, raffia and sunflower setting.

WAGON...WHOA! A big buffet table-turned-covered wagon fed hungry guests. Hearty chuck wagon cuisine was dished up on pie tins, and cowboy hats held snacks.

RAKING IN recollections of old-time weddings at the nostalgic site are the groom and best man, brother Dan.

Signs Pointed to Happy Trails...

Becky and Mike posted 12 road signs, similar to old Burma Shave ads, to direct guests to their wedding:

Point your wagons right this way.

'Cuz Mike 'n' Becky's gittin' hitched today!

The bride 'n' groom are so glad you came.

'Cuz without you it wouldn't be the same!

The chuck wagon's smokin'; the drinks are on ice.

The salads are chillin'; the chili's full of spice!

So aim straight ahead—yer almost there...

'N' the dress is casual, so watch what you wear.

Now turn 'round this corner—it's a tight squeeze.

And when you get here, show your invite, please.

Tie up your horses; park your carriage at the gate.

The weddin's getting started—dontcha be late!

This Couple's 'I Do's' Are In Red, White and Blue

THE CEREMONY in which Jill and Kevin Hestetune "got hitched" was as all-American as apple pie—complete with cowboys, cowgirls and a patriotic color scheme!

The striking wedding, which took place in early July in Soldiers Grove, Wisconsin, began as eight riders dressed in red, white and blue stepped their horses smartly through a series of precision maneuvers in the arena.

Moving in time to the music, the cowboys and girls created a spectacular star formation in the center of the ring...as some 300 guests in the grandstand clicked their cameras. Then a horse-drawn wagon entered carrying a pastor in a white robe.

The bride and groom trotted into the arena on horseback, circled it three times and joined the wedding party in the center of the ring to speak their vows.

"It was such a natural way for them to be married because Kevin and Jill do everything on horseback," confides the groom's mother, Darlene Hestetune. "They met on horseback. They go on trail rides and compete in rodeos and speed events. Kevin trains horses and Jill was a rodeo queen."

The patriotic theme included red, white and blue hues in many details—from the horses' leg wraps and the bride's boots to the wedding party's attire. Even the corsages were accented with stars and stripes ribbon. Sporting white shirts and hats, the bride and groom stood out from their party.

Practice made perfect for the big day. "The riders went through their routine twice before the wedding," Darlene remarks. "They were planning to do it faster, but when we realized the dust they'd create, we slowed it down. We also hosed down the arena just before the ceremony."

Afterwards, Jill and Kevin exchanged the traditional kiss, then made a not-so-traditional whooping exit at full gallop!

COUNTRY PRIDE was riding high on the day that Jill and Kevin Hestetune (above) got hitched. The bridal party donned patriotic duds, saddled up in an arena...and then hightailed it out at the end!

Photos: Joan Davig

Handy Twosome Builds on Romance

To begin building their new life, Amy Tussing and Michael Kennedy added some constructive touches to a Nebraska cabin site for their wedding.

Photos: Don Alderman/Alderman Photography

AT THE GATE, Amy Kennedy and husband Michael are off and running as a couple in Elmwood, Nebraska. "We built a Western-style lane marker by my parents' cabin where the wedding was set," Amy pens.

A FAMILY AFFAIR. With the bride's twin, groom's brother, nieces and nephews attending, the wedding was relatively perfect. "Mom made our dresses and helped me cross-stitch the ring bearers' pillows," Amy comments.

DANCING FOR ROMANCE. In the barn loft, a high-stepping time was had by the newlyweds and their guests. Rural mementos served as sentimental centerpieces and family wedding photos hung on the walls.

A SITE FOR LOVING "AYES" was the archway hammered together by the bride and groom. Amy's mom sewed the bright wedding banner.

HANDYMAN MAGIC. Michael, who works to win grins as a rodeo clown, also logged smiles from guests when they saw his handiwork, including a wagon card box. A neighbor made the pretty bows that flowed from the fence posts.

MOTHER NATURE presided when Daun and Russ Hembd wed beneath a rustic cedar cross in a picturesque pine grove. Towering trees on the couple's 80-acre farm formed a natural canopy for their open-air exchange of vows.

Couple Picks Country Cathedral in the Pines

THERE WAS no "needling" when Daun and Russ Hembd of Whitehall, Wisconsin decided to get married in a peaceful pine grove along a pasture on Daun's 80-acre hobby farm.

"Two rows of pine trees created a natural cathedral with a vaulted branch ceiling, green whispering walls and pine needle mosaic floor," Daun describes. "It was the perfect setting for our outdoor October wedding.

"To add to the natural altar, my father-in-law made a cross out of cedar boards and fastened it to a tree about 15 feet up, framed by pine boughs.

"Since we weren't sure how windy it might be, instead of lighting a unity candle, we decided to release two white doves," Daun recalls. "Unfortunately, we couldn't find any...but a neighbor raises white pigeons.

"When it came time to release the birds, Russ and I each tossed one into the air at the same moment. They went up and then nose-dived among the surprised guests! Luckily, no one, including the birds, was hurt."

Later, their feathered friends walked down the aisle side by side behind the last couple, raising chuckles from well-wishers who were seated on planks laid across straw bales.

Daun decked out her reception with a natural look as well. "We decorated a local club with grapevine bells, shocks of corn, baskets with dried flower arrangements (all grown on the farm), gourds, pumpkins and Indian corn.

"We'd gathered and pressed leaves, pine needles, moss and birch bark the fall before and used them to make programs, invitations and thank-you notes. After arranging them in a pretty way on card stock, we used clear Contact paper to hold them in place."

Hanging in a place of honor behind the tiered cake trimmed in autumn hues was a beautiful handmade quilt. "It contains 107 different squares shared by family and friends," Daun details. "It's now a treasured keepsake.

"It takes a lot of food to fill up 300 hungry guests," she adds. "Mom and Aunt Duke did most of the cooking. But all the hard work really paid off. We had a wonderful day."

One thing's for sure—Daun won't be looking back, pining for the kind of wedding she never had!

Their Day Blooms in Sunny Celebration

The forecast was bright for Lori and Lee Bischke's big day, with steady showers of happiness for this Canadian couple wed on the family farm.

Photos: Merle Damberger

SUITABLE FOR FRAMING. Split-rail fence and arbor made a picture-perfect backdrop for the bridal party. Lariat bouquets brought a country touch.

SUNNY FUTURE is what Lori and Lee Bischke look forward to in Stettler, Alberta. Sunflowers cast their wedding in a country light. Since couple takes a shine to horses, they used tack to decorate hall.

CLOSE COUNTS in the horseshoe table accent that Lee and Lori forged. He welded the metal candle holder, and she added a striking floral accent.

FIELDING A TEAM of well-wishers was a breeze with the wedding's informal air. Set on the groom's family farm, the ceremony was seasoned by bright sky, barn backdrop, lots of a-bale-able seats.

AN IN-JEAN-IOUS THEME of blue denim brought a casual look to her wedding, Lori writes. "Our heart-shaped cake was trimmed with denim ribbon to match the tablecloth and candles."

BEAMING BOUQUETS of sunflowers rose to the top of cream cans painted in a soft country blue. Lori gathered bunches of bulrushes, yarrow, tansy and grain from surrounding pastures to add a natural touch.

Wedding Is Homegrown in the Heartland

Farm-raised Briana Niemeyer and Jed Van Der Zwaag watched their love grow in the country...and decided it was good grounds for sharing a life together in Boyden, Iowa.

WALK IN THE PARK in Sioux Center, Iowa led to the spot where Briana and Jed Van Der Zwaag tied the love knot—literally—with rope her dad used to trim the arch he built, says the bride's mom, Marilyn, of Doon, Iowa.

FUN FODDER for conversation were straw bale displays at the reception in the community center, Marilyn says. "Friends and family loaned us their tack, plus we added boots and barbwire-bedecked fence posts."

OLD FLAMES ablaze in oil lanterns sparked the tables' Western flavor. Mini hay bales, hats and lassos tied into guests' place settings with bandanna napkins and feed sack nut cups. Bushel baskets held munchies.

Clark Studios, Orange City, Iowa

TO HAVE AND BEHOLD. Radiant Briana is a sight for Jed's loving eyes. She opted for a classic dress topped off with a mom-made hat. Her bright bouquet and other floral trims included a blend of garden buds and wildflowers.

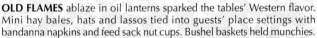

CUPID'S POSSE got their man *and* his blushing bride! The pint-sized ring bearer rang a cowbell while the flower girl dropped posies down the aisle.

Yankee Doodle Duo Says 'I Do!'

Declaring their love on the Fourth of July in Ft. Gibson, Oklahoma, Cheryl and Mike Owens pledged their allegiance to one another.

STAR-SPANGLED SWEETHEARTS Cheryl Moreland and Mike Owens wed in all-American style. Patriotic colors perked the party's outfits, silk flowers and bridal bouquet brimmed with cowboy hat trims.

A SLICE OF RANCH LIFE flavored the cake the groom's mom, Marie, made. "Mike and Cheryl raise cattle, so tiny horseshoe and lasso charms and 'barbwire' piping were perfect," she pens.

THE PORCH at an old military fort added a timeless feeling to the couple's wedding setting. A weathered wagon wheel, milk can, pillars and railing provided a nostalgic backdrop for bright blossoms.

BEAUTIFUL TO BOOT was the centerpiece made by a friend of the bride to keep in step with the Western theme. Her arrangement added a country touch to the dinner that highlighted smoked brisket.

TWO-STEPPING TWOSOME Tracy and Tom Noor share a kiss under a homemade sunflower-trimmed arch fashioned from hay bales. The Minnesota marriage was marked by a lively barn dance.

Wedding Has Barnyard Backdrop

IN THE HEART of Minnesota's dairy farming country, Tracy and Tom Noor put great stock in their marriage from the very start.

"Our wedding gifts included a calf from our neighbor and a piglet from my sister decked out in ribbons and bows," she chuckles from the wedding site, a family farm near Foreston she and Tom now call home. "The whole day was filled with fun-loving surprises."

Indeed, Tracy likens their country wedding to haying season. Everyone was ready and willing to pitch in!

"My mother-in-law and a friend fashioned an altar arch from hay bales and fencing wire," she tells. "They trimmed it with bandannas and wildflowers. Two 'honorary groomsmen' (wooden cowboy cutouts) added a touch of Western whimsy alongside.

"More blossoms spilled from a water trough planter in the haymow door...and filled calico-covered juice cans lining the aisle."

The ceremony was a genuine family affair with a dozen sisters and brothers in the wedding party. Luckily, the needle-sharp talents of a friend of the bride put everyone in country-style stitches.

"She accented my simple dress with fringe, lace sleeves and leggings and trimmed my hat brim with satin rosebuds," Tracy notes. "My bridesmaids wore peasant blouses and blue jean skirts. The guys looked handsome and relaxed in jeans, Western shirts and shoestring neckties.

"As I walked down the aisle, I took two roses from each of my bridesmaids to make my bouquet. Half the flowers were red for love, and half were white for serenity."

The open-air reception that celebrated their union was "relatively" perfect, Tracy enthuses. "Our photographer was Tom's cousin, my brother and niece were our DJ's and our aunts and uncles prepared the food.

"The bunkhouse doubled as a makeshift buffet hall where we served up roast pork, smoked turkey, wild rice and hot dishes."

The evening kicked off with a rafter-rattling barn dance as guests commenced to two-step by moonlight. "Everyone had such a good time," Tracy adds. "Tom and I have hosted a picnic every August since then."

In between anniversaries, they have lively reminders of their wedding day as close as their barnyard. "We've named that wide-eyed gift calf 'Heart', and our pig is 'Buddy'," Tracy confides with her brightest farm wife smile.

Duo Corrals Rural Nuptials

*Spurred on by a mutual love for ranch life,
Cynthia Malchow and Gary Wiggins herded
plenty of Western fixin's into their Colorado "I do's".*

MOUNTED atop this sweet cake was a rural scene rustled up by Jeanette from rope, dried flowers, mini hats and a tiny fence. Groom Gary added a good luck touch with a silver horseshoe he tacked onto the arch.

EASY DOES IT. Comfort was at the heart of the get-ups for Cynthia, Gary and their bridal party, from blue jeans to cowboy boots. The setting was relaxing as well. "They exchanged their vows in our own backyard," notes Cynthia's mom, Jeanette, from Castle Rock, Colorado.

BOOT BOUQUET. "We placed water glasses in cowboy boots and filled them with beautiful flowers and dried weeds," jots Jeanette. Gary, who's a custom bit and spur maker, created the conchos on the bouquets.

HAY—IT'S OFFICIAL! The signing of the marriage license took place on top of stacked bales. "Cynthia and Gary didn't even set a date until after the hay was in," grins her mom, Jeanette.

A RURAL FLAVOR extended to the reception with a down-home buffet. Small bales of hay and blue bandannas helped gussy up the food spread. Utensils were wrapped in napkins and tucked into gray enamelware.

Their Wedding Setting's a Thing of the Past

Knowing a modern service wouldn't do, Tina and Nicholas Wise chose to turn back the clock at a nostalgic chapel in Florida before heading toward the future together.

SHEDDING LIGHT on the union was a task mothers Beverly Wise (left) and Paula Crawford lovingly undertook. "The chapel has no electricity, so we brightened it with candles for a romantic look," Beverly tells.

HISTORIC HAPPINESS was assured for newlyweds Tina Conner and Nick Wise when they were wed at a living history museum in Silver Springs, Florida. "The one-room church was so simple and country," notes Nick's mom, Beverly.

ALTAR-ATIONS. To accent the altar, Beverly garnished it with garlands of flowers, candles and a cross she fashioned from red roses. Nick's grandmother, Jeanne, helped make the charming floral arrays.

HIS SUNDAY BEST was what minister Freeman Godwin wore to marry the pair in an old-time wood church he built.

A HISTORY LESSON. Their wedding site was the replica of a "cracker" church, so named after early ranchers who would herd cattle by cracking their whips overhead.

Riding Arena's the Site for Celebration

SPURRED on by her girlhood dreams, Amy Jo Radunz was determined to start off her married life with Patrick on stable ground.

"Growing up in the saddle around my grandparents' riding stable, I knew I wanted to get married there one day," she relates from her home in rural Mankato, Minnesota.

Thus, on a sun-kissed August afternoon, guests rounded up at Harvey and Alvera Brooks' horse farm for a North Country wedding with a definite Western accent.

"The procession was led by two horses, of course—then came our flower girl and ring bearer. Dressed as a junior bride and groom, they innocently stole the show!" Amy Jo chuckles.

"My mother had her hands full, sewing identical satin and French lace dresses for little Danielle and me, along with Western skirts and peasant blouses for my attendants.

"She also arranged the silk roses in our bouquets to carry the wedding theme colors—white, fuchsia and teal."

Waiting in the wings were two "special guests" who became a highlight of the simple ceremony. "Pat and I released a pair of white doves as symbol of our love and devotion," Amy Jo noted with a smile.

"Afterwards, our youngest attendant made a cute 'getaway' on horseback... and my grandfather gave Pat and me a ride in his antique carriage down the 'aisle' between towering pines."

The reception, held in the stable's indoor arena, was a family affair, she shares. "My six uncles used a front end loader to hang crepe paper streamers from the rafters.

"Meantime, my grandmother and aunts were busy making ham sandwiches, baked beans and salads. Mom baked a three-tiered cake accented with silk flowers to match our bouquets."

That evening, family and friends danced off their dinners to the toe-tapping tunes of a live country band playing atop a hay wagon.

"We were all amazed when the dove we'd released earlier flew into the arena and perched on a beam near the head table," Amy Jo cheerfully conveys. "We took it as a good omen when they stayed and cooed the night away."

BRIDLED AND GROOMED horses helped carry off Amy Jo and Pat Radunz's day. Her mom made the cake, and uncles trimmed the arena. Junior bride and groom (below) almost stole the show!

Christopher Kight Photographers

Kate Wolff

Hitched

FROM THIS DAY FORWARD...the fun's just beginning for these country-loving newlyweds. Clockwise from top right: Lori and Tom Shepish from Mastic, New York take a quick wedding siesta; bride Anna Boyd is in the driver's seat, while husband Joseph's riding high on the new tractor she bought for the couple's Schulenburg, Texas farm; Joanne and Stu McMahon are going with the grain in a wagon decorated with wheat and canola from their Galahad, Alberta acres; Jennifer and Brandt Anderson, Marysville, California, were easy to spot in a "mooving" getaway car.

. . . Happily Ever After

Index

Food

Crafts

Planning a 'Centsible' Wedding

Terri Brooks, mother of Amy Jo Radunz (see feature p. 112), used to manage a bridal shop. Here are her tips for an economical, time-saving wedding.

♥ Start planning as soon as possible after setting the wedding date. Research and shop to determine your options.

♥ Keep alert for sales at craft outlets, paper goods stores and businesses that carry merchandise in bulk.

♥ Use your imagination to see how everyday objects can be useful. Paper tablecloths can serve as wallpaper to brighten up a barn-turned-banquet hall, a barrel can hold a guest book, a hay wagon can double as a bandstand, etc.

♥ Welcome family and friends' offers to help. Folks who enjoy cooking, music, flower arranging or sewing will likely be honored to share their talents.

♥ Get the wedding party involved. Hold crafting bees and invite your bridesmaids to help make favors and decorations for the reception.

♥ Bake a modest-sized decorated cake for display and simple sheet cakes in different flavors to provide the necessary number of servings.

♥ Decide if you want formal wedding photos, relaxed candids or a combination and where you'd like them taken. Prepare a list of shots for the photographer to save time and money.

♥ Holding a wedding at a family home/farm can save rental fees…but make sure your setting is compatible with the size of the bridal party and guest list, seating, decorations and accessibility for guests.